UnStuck

The Owner's Manual to Success

Dr. César Vargas

UNSTUCK
The Owner's Manual to Success

Published by Veritas Invictus Publishing
8502 East Chapman Avenue # 302
Orange, California 92869

www.VeritasInvictusPublishing.com

ISBN: 978-0-9846837-3-4

10 9 8 7 6 5 4 3 2

Collection © 2011 Cesar Vargas, Ph.D., Michael Stevenson, Jason West, Susan Gole, Jeanne Munsell, Ronald Berg, Anita Thomas, Cathy Meyers and Val Rensink.
All Rights Reserved.

No part of this text may be reproduced, stored in a retrieval system, or transmitted by any means, electronic, mechanical, photocopying, desktop publishing, recording, or otherwise, without permission from the publishers. No patent liability is assumed with respect to the use of the information contained herein. While every precaution has been taken in the preparation of this book, the publisher and author assume no responsibility for errors or omissions. Neither is any liability assumed for damages resulting from the use of the information contained herein.

Table of Contents

Foreword 4

Chapter One: Getting Unstuck 5

Chapter Two: Cause and Effect 14

Chapter Three: Motivation for Success 27

Chapter Four: Creating Relationships for Success 35

Chapter Five: Getting from No to Yes 43

Chapter Six: Chunking for Success 53

Chapter Seven: Turn on Your Personal Television! 60

Chapter Eight: States and Anchors 69

Chapter Nine: Making Your Goals SMART 78

Chapter Ten: Tapping into Success 94

Bonus Chapter 101

Foreword

✦✦✦

In January of 2011, I was part of a top-secret business success training for NLP trainers in Orange County, CA. The topic of the training program was on how to be successful in the field of personal development trainings.

We expected to come in and learn how to hold events, how to do marketing, how to close the sale and other such topics. Little did we know we were going to do something far more special and far-reaching.

That sense of excited anticipation that I experience at the onset of every training turned into a vision of possibility and significance when Michael, our Master Trainer, essentially opened the class with, "So, who wants to write a book?"

It is because of the principles in this book that we, the authors, have all achieved the success we have now. We have not only used this information for ourselves, but helped to transform the lives of others with it. I think I speak for the group when I say that we all believe our purpose is to share this with others and transform the world one person at a time.

It is my hope that transformation begins with you, as you read these pages.

If you'd like to learn more about how to transform your life, visit my website at www.lifeunstucknow.com

Cesar Vargas, Ph.D.

January 2011
Orange County, CA

CHAPTER ONE:

Getting Unstuck

by Michael Stevenson

If you've been around self-help for even a short time, I know you've heard the name Napoleon Hill – the "guru" of self-development. Napoleon wrote one of the most read books of all time, "Think and Grow Rich."

If you only know the surface story of Napoleon, you might think that he was born rich, or born positive, or given some advantages that others weren't. That couldn't be further from the truth.

You see, Napoleon was at one point a simple reporter. He was a family man, married with a disabled son who was born without ears. They were not wealthy. As matter of fact, life was quite challenging in those times.

Andrew Carnegie, on the other hand, was the richest man in the world. He had amassed a fortune unlike anything seen in the modern world, and he built it all from scratch.

Carnegie knew how he had created his own fortune, and he had a notion that if you were to interview self-made millionaires, you would find they had all used the same principles and methods as he.

He believed that if someone interviewed these people they could construct a model for success that could be used to make one rich and also be taught to others.

A lot of study has been done on successful people, and they found out three things that are common to *all* of them.

1. Successful people make lots and lots of decisions.

Successful people are always making decisions. You don't find them sitting around, thinking about success. They're constantly taking action and making decisions that move them forward. There is a direct correlation between how many decisions you make in a day and how successful you are, and Carnegie knew this.

2. They make their decisions quickly.

Successful people don't hem and haw over their decisions. They take a very active approach to life and realize that there's no time to waste. They make decisions almost impulsively, trusting their gut without focusing much on the risk. As a matter of fact, successful people are always taking risks.

The difference in attitude between the successful and the unsuccessful is this:

Unsuccessful people spend their life using the following strategy, "Ready, aim… aim… aim… aim… aim…" They're so afraid of not hitting the target (or even the bull's eye), that they never actually pull the trigger. They spend their lives thinking about achieving their dreams, until they realize they've run out of time.

On the other hand, successful people take the following approach to life, "Ready, FIRE, and aim!" They take a shot, pull the trigger and find out what results they get. Then, based on those results, they adjust and fire again.

3. Once they start on a path, they *always* finish.

> Finally, successful people just don't give up. Thomas Edison, for instance, failed at many of his first attempts at the light bulb. A newspaper reporter once asked Edison, "You've failed seven hundred times to make a light bulb. How does that make you feel?" Edison replied, "I have not failed 700 times. I have not failed once. I have succeeded in proving that those 700 ways will not work. When I have eliminated the ways that will not work, I will find the way that will work."
>
> Most people would have given up after the first few tries, determining that they're not good enough. It isn't worth it. It's not the right time, or it's just not "in the stars." Edison knew that persistence equals success.

Carnegie sent Napoleon Hill a telegram, asking to see him in his office. This was a dilemma, because Napoleon had only enough money for two train tickets – one ticket there, and one ticket home. However, he knew if Andrew Carnegie was requesting his presence, it must be important, so he booked the train.

Now, when most people are faced with a task like that, they usually come up with some obstacles. The two biggest things that keep them from achieving their dreams are, of course, lack of time and lack of money – or at least a perceived lack.

Now, here's the question. If you had the opportunity to invest yourself in finding out the science of success, so that when you were done you'd be GUARANTEED (meaning, a certainty) to have all the knowledge and resources to become successful in all areas of life; you would do it, wouldn't you? Absolutely!

Now, Carnegie was a smart man, and he wanted to see how committed Napoleon was to taking on this task, so he threw the first obstacle at Napoleon.

He said, "Napoleon, this is no small task. This will likely take a 20 year commitment. However, I guarantee, when you're done, you'll have more resources than any other man on the planet in terms of becoming rich and successful."

Now remember, successful people always do three things: They make lots of decisions, they make them quickly, and once on the path, they always finish.

So Carnegie carefully watched his reaction. He realized that time wasn't the only obstacle people have to overcome. So he threw the second obstacle at Napoleon.

He said, "Not only that, but you'll have to pay your own way. I will not fund this project, so the commitment of your time and your money are entirely yours."

You see this was not purely an academic task. Carnegie's requirement was that the man who took this task would need to apply in himself, the principles, he learned to himself along the way. And he was sure that if Hill did this, he would become a millionaire before the end of the process.

Carnegie said, "I can promise you one thing. If you take this task, I will put you in touch with the first of these most successful people – myself. I will arrange for you to have full access and to take as much time as you need with me. After that, it's up to you."

"So, here's the opportunity of a lifetime. This is the chance to take a task and learn about how to create unlimited, wild success, and even teach it to others." Do you think if Napoleon had let those typical obstacles come into his mind that he would have said yes? Do you think if he said,

"What if I run out of money?" or "What if I can't find the time?" that he would ever have been successful?

If Napoleon Hill had allowed those doubts to creep into his mind, he would have been stuck in what we call, "The Comfort Zone."

The Comfort Zone

The Comfort Zone is the area of life where nothing happens. It's an area we spend a lot of time in.

It's the area of life where things aren't all good, but they're not all bad. A friend of mine calls it the "Land of blah, blah, blah…" I also often call it, "The Gray Zone," because it makes for such a bleak life.

The Comfort Zone includes everything that you have in your life right now, the good things, the not-so-bad things, and those things you'd rather not think about.

Most people live their lives clinging to this Comfort Zone because, even though their life isn't the way they want it to be, they've become used to it, or comfortable with it.

As a matter of fact, they've become so used to it that, when something better comes along, they're often afraid to take the step out of their Comfort Zone and they miss the opportunities.

They go through their life almost as if they're a pinball in a cosmic arcade machine. It's as if, one day, the Universe pulls the plunger back and pops them out of the chute into life. They bounce off of whatever stands in their way, constantly being bounced around, making a lot of noise, but not making a lot of difference in the direction they're moving. And finally, at the end, they drop down the big black tunnel.

That's no way to live life!!

The fact is you've got a choice, but you have to exercise that choice to have those things you want in life.

If all the things you dream about were in your Comfort Zone, you'd have them already. However, the fact is all the best stuff in life lies outside of the Comfort Zone. If there are things in life you want, that you don't have right now, you're going to have to step out of the Comfort Zone to get them.

Taking action is often uncomfortable when you're not used to taking action. We tend to cling so much to the familiar that stepping outside of the Comfort Zone sometimes seems impossible.

Nevertheless, you can develop a habit and even a taste for doing it, and the rewards are absolutely worth it. The more you step out of your Comfort Zone the better your life becomes, and the easier it is to step out.

T. Harv Eker, author of *Secrets of the Millionaire Mind*, actually goes as far as saying, "Your wealth is directly proportionate to your Comfort Zone."

Think of the most successful people you know. People like Bill Gates, Warren Buffet, Donald Trump, Michael Jordan, Oprah Winfrey, Thomas Edison, Albert Einstein, and even Napoleon Hill didn't make it big by playing it safe. They got out of the Comfort Zone. They took risks, they played big, and they won big.

Did any of those successful people ever stumble, fall, or "fail"? Of course they did! And that's *why* they're successful.

I often say, I'd rather learn from someone who has made all the mistakes and won, than a person who had it easy or was handed their success and never stumbled. Mistakes equal wisdom, and that's often as valuable as – or more valuable than – the successes, themselves.

The Problem with Comfort Zones

The real problem with Comfort Zones is this: As long as you continue to do what you've always done, you'll continue to get about the same results as you've always gotten.

If you're completely happy in life and could not want for more, quit reading this book – it's not for you.

However, if you'd like to have more love, happiness, health, success, money and other wonderful things in your life, you're in for an amazing journey because the authors in this book are *experts* at creating positive changes.

You're going to learn ways to change your feelings, to change your beliefs, to take action and to step out of the Comfort Zone in a BIG way.

Over a decade ago, I was stuck in my own Comfort Zone. As a child, I had always wanted to have a career helping people. I was sure I would grow up to be a doctor, a lawyer, a policeman or fireman. It didn't really matter to me what profession, as long as it was a helping or healing profession.

Nevertheless, while growing up, I found succeeding in education was harder and harder. Transitioning from elementary school to junior high was a challenge, and the transition from junior to senior high seemed to have done me in for good. I struggled and barely made it. My dreams of helping others seemed to have been shattered with no clear path or desire for continuing on through college at that time.

I'm now sure that if I had been taken to a psychiatrist as a young boy, they would have declared me to be ADHD and learning disabled, and put me on some mind-numbing drug like Ritalin. Thankfully, that never happened.

I eventually settled for a technical career, which I had a natural aptitude for, but no passion. While I did achieve monetary success in the software industry, I was completely unfulfilled and always longing for a greater purpose.

It wasn't until I quit smoking in 1998 that the spark of passion was lit inside of me. One simple hypnosis tape that I bought at the county fair changed my life, and I had found my purpose.

Was it uncomfortable for me to walk away from a six-figure salary, benefits, a regular paycheck and a stable job? You bet.

Did I take a risk in doing so? Totally.

Was it worth the risk? Absolutely.

The fact is, because I took a step out of the Comfort Zone, I will never have to look back on the years since then with regret and say, "I wish I had only…"

We only get one shot at each day, and every day you spend not doing what you want, not having what you want and not being who you want to be is a day wasted and gone. You must choose to step out of the Comfort Zone to live the life you desire.

So here's the opportunity of a lifetime.

When Napoleon listened intently to Andrew Carnegie offering the chance to take a task and learn about how to create unlimited, wild happiness and success do you think he asked himself, "What if I run out of money?" or "What if I can't find the time?" or "What if I fail?"

If he had allowed those thoughts to creep into his mind, do you think he would have had any measure of success? I think not.

Carnegie was a smart man, and he knew that successful people make lots of decisions, make them quickly, and always finish the path. So Carnegie had a stopwatch hidden under the desk in his lap.

At the moment, he posed the question, "So, are you up to it or not?" Carnegie clicked the stopwatch into action and unbeknownst to Napoleon

Hill, he had sixty seconds to answer. If he had taken even a tenth of a second longer, he wasn't the right man, and the offer would have been off the table.

As the story goes, it took him only about 20 seconds to answer and the rest is history. Napoleon Hill did find the secrets of success and did become a millionaire himself helping to create thousands of other millionaires along the way, even after his death.

You have opportunities like that. The question is: Do you make the decisions in that moment you have them, to do what is required, to live out your dreams?

You're reading this book for a reason. I don't know what that reason is. I don't know the fires that burn inside you. However, I do know that you have them for a reason, and you deserve them. That's what this book is about.

As you read this book, keep in mind the three things that will make you successful as you learn about the secrets of becoming "Unstuck," and put those secrets into action. Make lots of decisions, make them quickly, and finish what you start.

Michael Stevenson is a certified trainer, therapist and coach in Orange County, California. He is the author of *Learn Hypnosis... Now!* (www.learnhypnosisnow.com) and the creator of Hypnotic Trancescapes (www.trancescapes.com). He's the President of Transform Destiny, Inc. where you can take his online and live courses in success, motivation, hypnosis, NLP and more.

Get a free copy of Michael's best-selling book, *Learn Hypnosis... Now!*, when you sign up for his newsletter at www.transformdestiny.com/newsletter.asp.

CHAPTER TWO

Cause and Effect
by Jason West

"Every person creates for themselves the world in which they choose to live, and only they can change it. "

- Jason West

Reality

Since the dawn of mankind, philosophers have pondered the existence of reality. Are we really here? What is reality? Am I experiencing the same reality that everyone else is? What if everything we think, see, and feel are all just a big dream, and we are really just living in a catatonic state in some pod providing life energy for an alien life form...

Oops, I think I was wandering into a Matrix tangent for a moment, but really...how do we know what is real and what isn't? Fortunately, for us, we are living in an age where we are making new discoveries; an age of quantum physics, a time when we are just on the cusp of answering many of these questions of life and existence. At the time of this writing, an organization known as CERN in Geneva, Switzerland, was running experiments in the world's largest particle accelerator known as the Large Hadron Collider. This experiment was expected to provide evidence of the Higgs Boson, or the 'God Particle', which is theorized to hold all matter, and indeed the entire universe together. In addition to all the answers quantum physics has been providing about reality as we know it, this experiment has opened up even more mysteries that we have yet to answer.

One of these mysteries that has baffled scientists (and was even rumored to have confounded Einstein so much that he nearly left the field of quantum mechanics), was the famous Double Slit Experiment. While it is far too complex to explain fully in the confines of this book, the highly simplified version is when scientists shot electrons through an object with two slits cut into it, the resulting pattern left where the electrons would pass through the slits under normal circumstances leave a certain shape, but when the process was observed it would leave an entirely different shape.

What it proved was that the simple act of observing something could actually change the results you get in contrast to not observing it at all. It gives you pause for thought when you think of the old question "If a tree falls in a forest, but no one is there to hear it, does it make a sound?"

This fascinating paradox affects the world as we know it, and more importantly, it affects us individually in a profound way. The reality that we know and are familiar with is our reality because we are observing it as such. There are other realities that are not 'our reality', simply because we are not observing them. What this posits is that we can actually change our reality by observing a different reality!

History is littered with examples of people who view their realities differently. Let's take a look at a real life example: Donald Trump. Donald Trump is well known as one of the most successful and richest business people in modern times. However, did you know that he's filed for bankruptcy three times in his life? Now, for many people, bankruptcy is the end game, and people will normally quit and lose their dream, but not Trump. He has a different view on life, and he is simply not able to view his life as anything but being rich. And that has become his reality. I know that if he were to lose all of his money today, he would be back making millions within a couple of years. It is just who he is.

This is why for the majority of people living, they don't wander far in financial terms from the way they grew up – if they grow up poor, they will likely spend their adult years being poor, middle class people will normally end up middle class people, and the same goes for wealthy people. They are unable to see themselves living a life any differently. This also explains why the majority of lottery winners typically end up in the same place financially. In their mind, they still see themselves in the reality that they originally created for themselves.

The exciting news about all of this is what this means for your life. If you can change the way you view your reality, you can literally create a new reality for yourself. If you change the way you look at relationships, you can have the relationship you've always dreamed of. If you change the way you look at your health, you can have the body you've always dreamed of. And best of all, if you change the way you think about money, you can have the wealth of your dreams!

This is the guiding principle behind Napoleon Hill's book "Think & Grow Rich", which has single-handedly created more millionaires than any other piece of literature on the planet. Ask any wealthy person you know, and they will certainly tell you that the principles behind their success are the same principles mentioned in that book.

This is also the guiding principle behind "The Secret" and the Law of Attraction movement that has recently been popularized in much of today's society.

Easy, right? Well obviously if it were that easy, we'd all be millionaires! That's because in order to see things in a certain way, we have to believe them to be a certain way – it's all fine and dandy to say we believe something, but to truly believe it requires many changes in our thinking and attitudes. Things we often find ourselves getting stuck in every day.

So how do we 'unstick' ourselves and change our beliefs? This is where the power of Neuro Linguistic Programming (NLP) comes into play. With NLP, we can actually pinpoint the beliefs we possess, and using the various techniques of NLP, we can begin to change those beliefs so that we see reality the way we want to see it.

NLP Model of Communication

Neuro Linguistic Programming (NLP) is a series of processes designed to use the basic language of our mind to achieve the results we want in life. It was founded by Richard Bandler and John Grinder in the 70's as they studied successful people in their chosen fields and modeled their behavior. They believed that if you could emulate the behavior of a successful person, then you would naturally obtain the same results as that person. They created a system of techniques that enables people to break down and model the behavior of other successful people. In particular, they chose to focus on the world of therapy and modeled some of the renowned therapists of the time such as Milton Erickson, Fritz Perls, and Virginia Satir, although the same processes can be (and are) applied to other fields such as sales, writing, teaching, etc.

In order to understand NLP, it is necessary to understand how our mind works and processes information. Our mind takes in all information via our five senses: Eyes (visual), Ears (auditory), Feelings (kinesthetic), Nose (olfactory), and Mouth (gustatory).

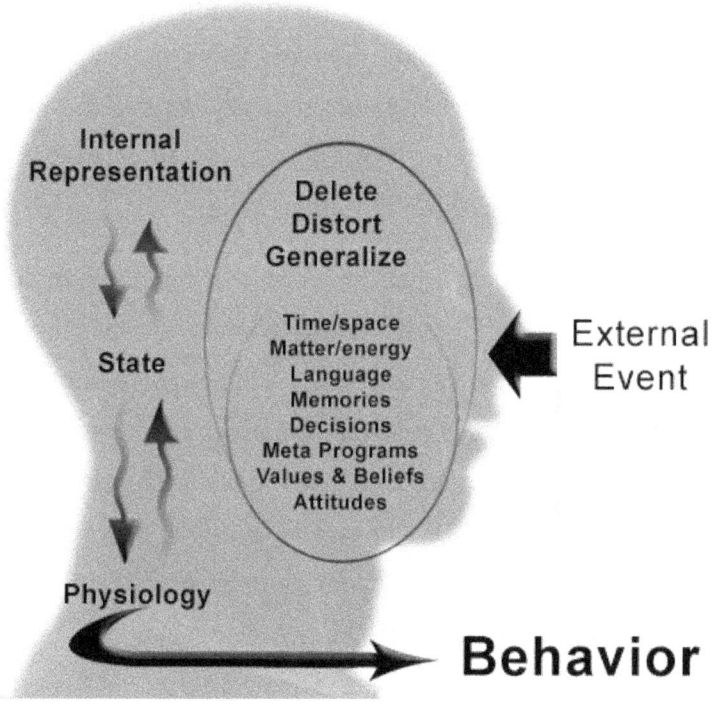

We have a LOT of information coming in through our senses at any given moment in time. In his book "Flow", Mihaly Csikszentmihalyi explains how we take in approximately 6 million bits of information in any given second. Unfortunately (or maybe fortunately) for us, we are only able to process and assimilate 128 bits of that information at any given moment. That would be the equivalent of us taking in and processing one word out of about 200 average sized books. This minuscule amount of information that we process forms reality as we know it. All the rest of the information that comes in through our senses forces the mind to delete, distort, and generalize information in order to process and make sense of it.

By deleting information I mean that the mind deletes things it knows it will not use, like all the license plate numbers of all the cars that drive past you on the freeway. Your mind automatically deletes the humming sound that your computer makes. That information did enter our minds, but our mind automatically deleted that information.

By distorting information, I mean that our minds will often add or subtract or otherwise change things in order for it to make sense. There is an interesting phenomenon known as the McGurk Effect which illustrates this beautifully. It describes how your vision of something affects what you hear. A demonstration of this effect (you can find it on YouTube by searching for McGurk Effect) shows a man repeatedly speaking the sound "Bah." After several times of this, he begins speaking the sound "Fah." It is later explained that in the second cut where he began speaking "Fah", they only changed the video portion of it, but not the audio so that the lips appeared to be including an "F" sound. The man was in actuality still saying "Bah" although you 'hear' "Fah." Even after watching the video several times, I still would swear that I heard something I actually did not hear. Distortion is the phenomenon that is the cause of faulty eyewitness memories that lead to false convictions. Of the more than 200 wrongful convictions that were later overturned due to DNA evidence, 75% were convicted based on erroneous eyewitness identification. Who knows how many thousands of people are wrongly convicted of crimes they never committed because someone's mind rejected what it did, in reality, see?

When your mind generalizes information, it bundles information together to take it in. When you drive by a bunch of trees, you don't see the individual leaves, but rather a mass of green. When we read, we don't really pay attention to the individual words, but rather clusters of words that form sentences. This phenomenon allows us to enjoy movies that appear as if they are moving in real life motion, although, in reality, we are looking at individual pictures, being flashed before us at 24 frames per second.

If we didn't delete, distort, and generalize, we would literally go insane. Think of all the times you have said that you're mentally overloaded…and then multiply that by a few hundred thousand! Of course we all delete, distort, or generalize different things, and this is what makes us all unique. In NLP, we call these "filters".

We all look at life through different filters, giving us different perspectives on life as we know it. It gives us different realities. What's real for one person might not be real for someone else. Which is why two people, from exactly the same upbringing, going to the same college, and starting off with the same amount of money can turn out so differently. One might end up a multi-millionaire, while another can wind up in prison for theft. Different Realities!

All of these things our mind allows in is in order to process from the core of who we are – our identity. The way we view time and space, the way we communicate using language, our decisions, our strategies for dealing with life, our beliefs and values are determined by what we have filtered into our minds. We call this our "Internal Representation".

Our Internal Representation of life determines the state that we are in. If one is depressed, it is because the filters on life have created beliefs and attitudes that have put that person into a depressed state. Likewise, if you are happy, it is merely because your current beliefs and attitudes have created that state.

Our state can also be created through our physiology. That's right! You can actually control your state by putting yourself physically into the state. Your mental state will naturally follow. If you are not in a happy mood, you can literally force yourself to improve your mood by simply looking up and smiling for a few minutes. You can also do things that you would normally do when you are happy ... have sex, ride a roller coaster, spend time with your kids. Even if you are not happy now, you will become happy after just a few minutes of doing happy things. I challenge you, the next time you find yourself in a less than a desirable state, to do something physical that you normally do when you are in a better state, and notice how much better you feel. This is an amazing concept, because it means that we can always control how we feel. Unfortunately, physiological state control is only temporary…when you exit that physiology; you will no longer be in that state.

Your State Determines Your Behavior

No matter which way you achieve your state, either by internal representations or by physiology, you will behave accordingly. If you are in a lazy state of mind, you will find yourself doing lazy things… lying around on the couch, watching TV, or doing nothing. If you are in a positive motivated state, you will find yourself productive and getting things done. Have you ever been to a Tony Robbins or other motivational seminar? They spend an entire weekend motivating you and pumping you up. When you get home, you are in an amazing state - writing down goals, getting yourself organized, and being incredibly productive…only to have that state wear off in about a week or so and going back to your normal routine.

You've gone back to your normal, everyday state. What if there was a way to control your state in a more permanent fashion? The wonderful thing about NLP is that it allows you to change your internal representations, which create the state that you are in. Your beliefs, attitudes, and values are not temporary. If you can change your beliefs about what makes you happy or sad, then you can learn to be in a state of perpetual happiness! Likewise, if you can change your attitudes and beliefs about money by changing the attitudes you have about how important it is to save money and not waste money on frivolous things, you would find yourself in the state of someone who saves and is responsible with money. In that state, you will find yourself having much more of it!

Your Behaviors Lead to Results

Everything that you do in life leads to a certain result. If you are lazy all of your life and just do the minimum amount to get by, the resulting consequences of that behavior will be that you will go nowhere, live poorly, and always struggle to get by. On the contrary, if you stay productive, work hard, and save money – your results will be much more positive. This should be obvious to everyone, and you know it's true because we are always attempting to change our behavior to get a result. How many people do you know that go on a diet, so they will get that body that they want? They have a result that they want to achieve, and they know that the only way to achieve that result is to eat less. Unfortunately, we all know how most diets work out. These people are forcing a behavior without changing their state. You can only force a behavior for so long through sheer willpower. People still want to eat the forbidden foods because they are in a state that wants to eat them. And the best way to change that state is by changing their internal representation about the way they think about food.

Cause and Effect

Want to know the real secret to success in anything in life? If you apply this principle in any endeavor you do, you are virtually guaranteed that you will achieve a high level of success. This principle is applied by every successful person, regardless of whether they are aware of it or not...it is the principle of Cause and Effect.

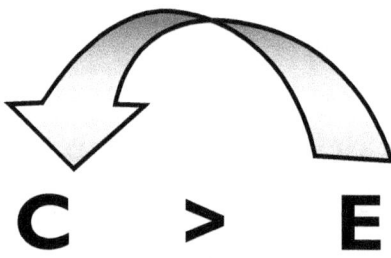

This principle states that for every Effect, or result, there is a directly correlated Cause. Whenever you do something (or don't do something) there will be a result that occurs because of your action (or inaction). When I clean my kitchen at home, the result is that my kitchen looks neat and orderly. If I choose not to clean my kitchen, the result is that the dishes begin to pile up, and the kitchen becomes messy. When the kitchen becomes messy, it is only because I didn't do anything about it – I was the 'cause' for the kitchen getting messy. I could make excuses and blame others for piling up the dirty dishes, but the ultimate cause for a messy kitchen is that I chose not to clean it.

Let's take this even a step further now. Suppose I was not the one in command of cleaning the kitchen. It is somebody else's responsibility. Let's pretend that the kitchen once again gets messy. It's not your fault now, right? It is completely out of your control, and there is absolutely nothing that you could do to get a clean kitchen again, right? Wouldn't that be sad if that were the case...that we were completely helpless to get the result that we wanted? Fortunately, we can be at cause for the problem. There ARE things that we can do...we can clean the kitchen ourselves. We can have a talk with the person who is responsible for cleaning it. We can hire a maid. We can eat out every day instead of eating at home. Isn't it wonderful that we have so many choices available to us if we choose to be at cause for that problem?

In the biggest Fortune 500 corporations, the buck always rests with the CEO of the company. He or she is ultimately responsible for EVERY single thing that happens in the corporation. In April of 2010, an oil rig in the Gulf of Mexico exploded, killing 11 men and causing the biggest accidental oil spill in the history of the oil industry. Who do you think took the brunt of the criticism for the oil spill? That's right, Tony Hayward, the CEO of BP, was forced to resign from the company. Why? He is the one expected by the company shareholders to be at cause for every event that occurs within the BP Company. Did he cause the explosion? No. Did he have the ability to immediately stop the leak that devastated the Gulf of Mexico? No. Even so, his job was to make decisions.

A congressional investigation into the incident determined that, had more safety measures been put into place prior to the accident, the entire incident could have been avoided. Hayward had made a decision earlier to cut costs and make shareholders more money by not investing in those safety precautions. Had he been living at cause for everything in the company, then that accident would have been avoided.

Imagine the power and the choices you would have if you were living at cause for every single thing that happened in your life; the good and the bad. If you can be at cause, then suddenly you would be presented with more choices, more options to deal with all the things that come up in life. Not happy with the car you drive? If you are at cause, then you can find a solution. You can get another job to make money. You can get a loan. You can sell your old car and your stamp collection that you've had since you were a kid. There are unlimited possibilities, but you must first stop coming up with excuses and, instead, come up with choices. Not happy with your relationship? Instead of bitching about it, you can go to counseling, you can get a divorce, and you can work on yourself to become a better person.

The majority of people on this planet love to come up with excuses about why they can't do this or can't do that: I can't afford it, we don't have enough money, I don't have a proper education because my parents couldn't afford to send me to college, I can't make any sales because the leads my company gives me are all crap, I grew up in a poor neighborhood, so I don't have the proper etiquette and social skills to blend in with a higher caliber of people, or I have a job that I work at that doesn't give me time to go back to school.

All of these are examples of living in effect, instead of living at cause. The moment you begin to live at cause in your life is the moment you can begin to get what you want out of life.

I have a challenge for you. If you truly do it, you will begin to see choices you've never dreamed of spring up in your life, and you will begin to see a shimmer of light where before there was only darkness. For the next seven days, I challenge you to be at cause for EVERY SINGLE THING that happens in your life.

From your happiness at work, to your relationship with your significant other, to how much money is in your bank account, to the people who cut you off on the freeway, to any sickness you might be experiencing. EVERYTHING! If you are late for work because the traffic was really bad, ask yourself how you were at cause for being late...and what you can do to prevent it from happening next time.

If you come home and your spouse immediately begins to yell at you, ask yourself how you were at cause for that, and then ponder about what you can do to prevent it from happening next time.

But Jason, what about things that are truly out of your control? What if a baby is born with HIV? That's not the baby's fault is it? How can a person be born with HIV be at cause for that? We can go into extreme examples all day long...I am simply asking you to ponder how you can be at cause for it. As for the person with HIV, he can be at cause in one particular way: how he chooses to live life with it. He can have a good attitude about it, or a bad attitude about it. Science has shown that people with diseases, coupled with high levels of stress and negative emotions due to the disease progressively get worse. I remember reading one case of someone who acquired HIV, but was determined to live a better life because of it. He began exercising every day and changed his diet (he became a vegetable smoothie fanatic), and changed his outlook on life. One day, the doctors informed him that he was no longer carrying the virus!

A hypnotherapist I know has treated several people who were born with some sort of ailment. In nearly all the cases he's treated, during hypnotic age regression, the patients claim, they got the disease due to something they did in a past life.

Now whether you believe in past lives or not (I personally do not), it is still interesting to note. One very inspirational person whom I know of and admire greatly was born without any arms or legs due to a rare disorder known as Tetra-Amelia. Nick Vujicic chose to be at cause for his life. Instead of complaining and making excuses for why he can't do this or that (like nearly anyone else in his predicament would), he chose to focus on everything he could do. He taught himself how to write, type on a computer, play the drums, brush his teeth, comb his hair, swim and fish. Oh yes, he even plays golf! He is currently an evangelist and a motivational speaker, and runs an impressive non-profit organization "Life Without Limbs." The power you gain from being at cause for your life is limitless.

NO MORE EXCUSES and living in effect for your life. It is time for you to BE AT CAUSE, and achieve all the success and greatness you are entitled to!

Jason West, MNLP, MTT, MHt is a board certified clinical hypnotherapist, master NLP practitioner, trainer, success coach, award winning speaker, and the founder of MetaShifts Hypnotherapy and MetaShifts Research Center in Laguna Hills, CA.

Through his hypnotherapy practice, Jason is committed to helping people of all walks of life to bring about the positive change that they desire in their lives. Utilizing his advanced training in Neuro Linguistic Programming (NLP) and hypnosis; employing the knowledge and skills gleaned as a graduate of the Dale Carnegie Human Relations and Communication Course, Leadership Course, and Sales Training Course, as well as his experience coaching students going through the Dale Carnegie Courses; implementing his 11+ years of valuable business experience; pulling from his community involvement as a former president of the Rotary Club, and member of Toastmasters, Chamber of Commerce, and Business Networks International; exploiting his near obsessive compulsion to hone and refine his skills - always training and studying to improve his ability to help others; and taking advantage of his uncanny knack for guiding people in the direction they need to go; Jason is in a unique position to help you achieve the change you want in life. Contact him at **www.metashifts.com**.

CHAPTER THREE

Motivation for Success
by Anita Thomas

"How soon 'not now' becomes 'never'."

- Martin Luther

How many times have you started a project full of excitement, such as learning to golf or plant a garden, only to stop shortly after starting? You would think that being successful at reaching your goal and getting what you want would be enough to motivate you, but it hasn't been, has it? Even if an action or goal is positive in nature, it doesn't always mean you will be motivated to do it. You need a driving force, a strong desire to push you into action and to go through to completion. Motivation is a mental state that you can learn to get to whenever you need it.

There are books and seminars filled with strategies and techniques that all say they have the answer, but you can't even get yourself motivated to do that. Well, I love to read, so I've read a lot of the self-help motivational books, and I am a seminar junkie, so I believe in continuous learning. However, if you need a quick fix to get unstuck and motivated to take bigger actions to improve your life, I would like to suggest that you try one more process. You can learn some basic Neuro-Linguistic Programming (NLP) in literally minutes that can motivate you to be, to achieve and to have what you want.

I know it works because I see the benefit in my life as I use NLP technique to get tasks completed that I don't want to do. I use NLP techniques to motivate myself when my kitchen sink has no more room for another dirty dish and my walking shoes need a walk.

I am getting things done like never before (heck, I am contributing to a book). Using NLP strategies has changed how I live my life for the better, every day in every way. NLP helped me get unstuck, and I know it can do the same for you.

The motivation strategies taught in NLP are simple, powerful and effective ways to bring about permanent and immediate changes in your life. You have dreams and goals, things you want to have and get done. Well, getting motivated is an important step in getting to those perfect end-results you want. Learning some basic NLP is an easy and effortless way to experience and achieve those results.

Motivational Direction -- What's yours?

There are two primary motivational directions discussed in NLP. One is when you *move away* from something, such as "I can hear my partner yelling at me for wasting money on these $1,000 golf clubs I bought. I see a really ugly scene here that I would rather stay away from. Guess I had better finish those expensive private golf lessons I paid for in advance." The thought of the confrontation that will take place is something you might want to *move away* from. Is this you? Are you usually *moving away* from difficulties, pain, or uncomfortable situations?

The other type of motivation moves you *towards what you do want*. You really want to plant a vegetable garden. You think about how in a few months you will have fresh vegetables on your table for dinner. Everything in your salad will have been grown in your own garden. The tomatoes, cucumbers, and carrots, will taste really good and yours will be all organic without the extra cost. The thought of what you are going to get from finishing your garden pulls you *towards* the digging, planting and sweaty work needed to get your garden done. Is this you? Do you usually *move towards* what you want, your goals, the rewards and the feeling of accomplishment?

What's your primary motivational direction? Do you usually *move towards* pleasurable, enjoyable things you want or *away from* what you don't want such as disappointment, conflict, and discomfort? Your motivational direction is a mental process that affects how you live your life. To some degree you have used both as you move through your life. You know that the two directions can motivate you, and both are useful in different situations.

Neither direction is better than the other; they both offer benefits and disadvantages. There are times when in moving *away from* something like a destructive relationship or dangerous situation is the best action, just as there are positive relationships and situations worth *moving towards*.

If you are more often motivated by the "*away from*" direction, you may be a great problem solver, you may be motivated to fix things before they get worse, which would be a win for you. If you are *towards* motivated then your reward is getting to the goal.

People tend to use the same motivational direction for most things in their life. So, if you are one to say, "No, no, I don't want that, it bothers me, and there are some negative consequences that I don't want to deal with", you probably use "the *away from*" direction in most areas of your life. Consequently, if you *move towards* what you desire, you might say, "yes, this looks good, feels good, and I am going to enjoy this". This is most likely your usual motivational style.

Knowing your dominant motivational direction can help you become more successful in obtaining your goals with less effort and stress. The following are good strategies for you if you tend to *move away* from what you don't want. If you mostly use *away from* motivation you should pay attention to signs of discomfort and react quickly so that you have more choices and less stress.

Furthermore, be aware that as you *move away* from what you don't want, so does your motivation. By paying attention to your levels of anxiety, pain, and what you don't want you can take action sooner while you have some choice, before you experience a negative consequence. Remember that the direction you move in affects your life so pay attention to where you are going and how you get there!

Motivation and Procrastination

What is it you wish to motivate yourself to do today? What is it that you would like to accomplish, and that would improve your day or your life? What's your feeling about it? Do you have a strong or weak desire to achieve it? Do you have a strong desire to take action and get this thing done? Alternatively, do you kind-of, sort-of, maybe, want to do it today?

The Principle of Polarity says that everything is dual and has two poles. Motivation and procrastination follow this principle as does towards and away from the motivational direction, they both deal with your level of desire, and they only differ in the degree. More desire equals more motivation, and weaker desire is procrastination.

Let's say you have a pole with one end being a weak desire and the other end being a strong desire; you would find procrastination and motivation at opposite ends, they would differ only in degree of desire. If this is true then desire has two opposite poles. If the weak desire was at the bottom end of the pole, that's where you find procrastination at the bottom, then motivation would be at the top of the pole. If you have a strong desire or motivation to accomplish a task, then you would find yourself further towards the top end of your desire pole. When you are motivated, that's strong desire. If you are just not feeling it, your desire is weak, and you might be saying, "maybe I will" or "maybe I would", then you are moving down the pole towards less desire into procrastination.

You think about the aerobics class that is being offered at the gym this morning and that would be a nice start to your "giving back" 10 pounds to the universe program. Alternatively, it would be nice to get that report out of the way and get your boss off your back. However, it is such a nice warm sunny day. It's a perfect beach day to just relax and enjoy putting your feet in the sand. One of those really good sausage sandwiches while you sit in the sand would be so nice. Right now in your mind, the desire to relax at the beach is stronger than the desire to give something to the universe or a finished report for your boss.

So, if strong desire leads to motivation, how do you build your desire and get things done?

- To increase your motivation and get unstuck
- Connect your values to your goals
- Start with an image of the thing you desire
- Think about the benefits you will obtain with the successful achievement of your goal
- See the perfect-end-result of your goal accomplished
- Get the feeling of your goal already achieved

Values and Modalities

Your values influence your motivational desire and determine what things mean to you. Your values will determine which motivational direction you will go in order to reach your goal. You need to identify your most important values to gain the motivation to take action and to get what you want. You need to ask yourself, "What is it about this goal, thing, or want that is important and holds meaning for me?"

Do you value love, family, security or is your number one value creating financial freedom? Your values are how you measure your success and achievement of your goals. The stronger your values are, the stronger the motivation to reach your goals.

When you think of your strongest values and the experiences they create, you get a picture of what that looks like. In making that image you use your sensory modalities: auditory, kinesthetic, visual, olfactory (smell) and gustatory (taste). The use of these modalities and submodalities (the smaller more detailed parts within a modality) can increase your motivation by making the thought of the value of the experience or goal more compelling and desirable.

If you value family and enjoy holiday dinners with your family, when you imagine going to Christmas dinner to be with them, you probably use several modalities to think of this event. By making rich detailed pictures of what you value and want you can use these different modalities you will increase your motivation. If you turn up the color, brightness, and the sounds of laughter and happiness, and throw in the taste of your favorite foods that are on the table you can hardly wait to get there. You may not like the 25 mile drive but the high value you place on family and holidays may motivate you to get there. NLP strategies like the use of modalities and submodalities can enhance your desire to achieve your goals.

What will be the benefit or value of achieving your goals? In order for a goal to motivate you, it must have some level of pleasure or significance or benefit to you, personally. Unless you put some importance and value on the results, they won't have any motivational pleasure for you.

In other words, for the motivational pleasures you choose to be most effective they must:

- Be something you place significant personal value on
- Be something you believe is possible
- Happen immediately upon completion or shortly after the completion of the action or behavior

Setting Goals

When you consider all aspects of the goal, then why do you want this? What will be the benefits, the results from your successful achievement? Visualize what you are going to do and what your reality will look like after this goal is successfully completed.

The expected beneficial outcome of a goal can be used to help define a motivational desire. Your personal expectation, what you assume the results will be from taking a particular course of action plays a significant role in determining whether or not you move towards that goal or not. If you perceive that there will be an experience during or immediately after the completion of a goal that is positive and pleasurable, then desire will build.

So, let's build a powerful positive image for our perfect end-result. Make the picture dissociated (i.e. see yourself in the image), like on a television screen in full-blown color, surround-sound and vivid experience. You can even use the controls on your media system to make this a HD, blue-ray, 3-D experience with soundtrack. Now make this an awarding winning picture of your life event and future direction.

There are so many NLP patterns and strategies that can get you motivated in a few minutes. You could use chaining anchors to move from Procrastination to a Motivated State and see the perfect-end-result of your goal accomplished.

By using an NLP motivational strategy of setting a chain of anchors and then triggering them, you can quickly and easily visualize and feel your future success get motivated. This technique and many others can easily and effortlessly assist you to the successful achievement of your desires.

Discovering and using the strategies and techniques of NLP to reprogram my mind has produced amazing results for me. The dishes are washed and my contribution to this book was successfully completed this morning.

If you are not satisfied with your life and the way things are going then you might want to consider changing some of your past programming, and that's what NLP can help you do. If you want to get unstuck, take an NLP class and change your life quickly and easily.

Anita Thomas is a certified Neuro Linguistic Programming (NLP) Master Practitioner and Hypnotherapist in Los Angeles, California where she is a credentialed school guidance counselor and elementary teacher. She is also an entrepreneur and owns a fair trade business which can be found on the web at: www.fairworldtraders.com

CHAPTER FOUR

CREATING RELATIONSHIPS FOR SUCCESS

by Suzan Gole

Have you ever had a conversation with a person where you felt naturally 'in sync'? Perhaps it felt like you were connecting with your thoughts as much as with the words you used. That's what rapport feels like. It's easy to create rapport with individuals or groups of people, once you know how. The basic premise of rapport is:

"When people are like each other, they tend to like each other"

Rapport is an essential part of everyday life, whether interacting with family members, co-workers, or just the person behind the register at the market where you shop.

There are six ways to build rapport

1. **Match the other person's words:** We are likely to be drawn to people who are similar to us, so matching how a person behaves and thinks will create rapport. Matching the way a person speaks is also a great way to build rapport with them. The words people use will tell you what their sensory preference is; whether they process the world through such as visual (sight), auditory (sound) or kinesthetic (feeling). People have their own style of speaking with the use of similar words and phrases that make that person unique. Have you noticed a family member or a friend that uses a particular word(s)

or phrase all the time? I have a friend who loves using the word exquisite when describing things she likes and even actions "that home run was simply exquisite". We each have our own individual way of communicating. You just have to pay attention to people's words to hear that there are patterns and phrases that are unique to that person.

2. **Match the other person's physiology:** People who are in natural rapport typically match and mirror each other's body language. Matching the posture of the other person can make them feel more at ease. Copying the way they sit, their gestures, movements, facial expression or even their blinking, will cause their unconscious mind to recognize you as a similar person and create that rapport! You don't have to match them exactly, for example, if they are tapping their fingers, you could bounce your knee in a similar rhythm. Not only is this fun, but it really works and the person immediately feels a close connection to you.

3. **Match the other person's voice:** You can also match your voice to the tone, tempo, timbre or volume of the other person. Tone is the pitch of the voice. Tempo is the speed of the speech, Timbre is the quality of the voice, and volume is the loudness of the voice. If the person's speech is slow and deliberate, he will feel more comfortable with you if you're matching him at a slow and deliberate pace.

4. **Match the other persons breathing:** Matching breathing is a powerfully unconscious way of creating rapport. It comes from babies breathing in sync with their mothers in infancy. Breathe in when they are breathing and out at the same time, at the same speed. If you are speaking, breathe in when they breathe in, and speak when they're breathing out.

5. **Match how they handle information:** Some people are more detail-oriented while others prefer a bigger picture. If you mismatch a person's information processing style, you'll lose them quickly. Detail-oriented people will think you've got your head in the clouds and lack substance, if you speak in big-picture terms. Big picture thinkers will think you're boring and anal if you speak in detail-oriented terms. Match their processing style by listening to how they speak.

6. **Match common experiences:** People who have some common experiences, such as common interests, similar backgrounds or matching values or beliefs will often find some superficial rapport naturally. Suppose you meet a stranger who comes from your home town or went to your same alma mater. You'll quickly find yourself in a lively conversation, looking for more common experiences. This can also happen when you speak to a stranger and happen to have friends in common or meet a person on an airplane that is in the same line of work you are in.

To establish rapport you must be patient and a great observer. It's important to be subtle when using these techniques. You want the unconscious mind to see your rapport tactics, not the conscious mind. If you are mimicking the person overtly, and they become aware of it, you'll likely lose any rapport you've gained.

Practicing these skills

As with most things, you'll get better at this the more you use it, so it's important that you practice whenever possible. Practice building rapport with strangers at the mall or even in line at the grocery store.

Rapport is one of the main elements to NLP, Hypnosis, counseling and sales success techniques. No matter how knowledgeable or confident you are, whether you even have an excellent track record, you will be unable to make any kind of an impact with your prospective client if you are unable to gain rapport. Rapport is the foundation on which everything is built.

Mirroring

Mirroring is the act of subtly imitating a person's behavior and movement, as if they were looking into a mirror, reflecting their movements back to them. This must be done subtly. Unconscious, the other person feels accepted and appreciates your interest in them. You are mirroring that person's ongoing experience. Even though they may be unaware of your actions or intent, it will still have an amazing effect.

Mirroring the other person will create a positive feeling and response for both you and the others involved.

Matching

When matching another, you will subtly imitate the person using the same side of the body as them. If they gesture with their right hand, you use your right hand.

Often, mirroring is to make the effect even more unconscious. If the other person gestures while speaking, you can stay still until it's your turn to speak. Then, make your comments using the same or similar gestures.

Leading

Once you have rapport, you will be able to lead and they will unconsciously follow. To test your level of rapport, make a movement or gesture and watch to see if they follow. For example, you might scratch your head and then see if they do too.

Mismatching

You can also *break* rapport, if you so choose. For example, if you're speaking with someone who is rambling on, and on, and on, you may feel stuck. However, if you mismatch their physiology, voice and other characteristics, you'll break rapport with them. You'll be surprised how quickly and easily that conversation will end!

Modalities and How They Play a Role in Rapport

We experience and process the world through our senses, primarily, Visual (V), auditory (A), kinesthetic (K). These "modalities" are called representational systems (rep systems) because they are how we represent experiences in the mind.

Preferred Representational Systems

We each use a combination of our senses, contextually. However, you probably focus more on one of them. Each of us has this preferred representational system that we rely on more than the others.

When learning something new, for instance, some people prefer to see the task performed, some prefer to hear about how to do it, some prefer to get a feeling for it by doing it themselves, and some have to make logical sense of it.

Knowing there are different systems, I want you to be aware that none are any better than the others. Though, each preferred representational system will often tend to exhibit certain behaviors or personality traits.

The following are some general traits for each of the preferred representational systems. Remember, as with all generalizations, there are always exceptions.

Visual Traits

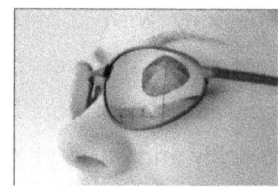

- Neat and orderly
- Speak quickly
- Likes visual art
- Organizers
- Planners
- Environmental
- Aesthetic
- Good spellers
- Good at visualizing
- Good visual memory
- Unaffected or not distracted by noise
- Good readers
- Often scribble, doodle or visualize when bored
- Forget to relay verbal messages
- Answer questions with a simple yes or no
- Sometimes tune out when they mean to pay attention

Auditory Traits

- Have conversations with themselves
- Often affected or distracted by noise
- Silently make words or whisper as they read
- Enjoy reading aloud and listening to audio books

- Great at telling details, but not as good at writing
- Speak rhythmically
- Like music, rhythm and other auditory pleasures (like the sound of rain)
- Learn by listening, and remember what was discussed
- Are talkative, love discussion, and go into lengthy descriptions
- Can spell moderately well, if they can sound the word out

Kinesthetic Traits

- Speaks slowly
- Respond to physical rewards and touching
- Touch people to get their attention
- Stand closer than most
- Are physically oriented and move a lot

- Memorize by doing
- Use a finger as a pointer when reading
- Gesture more than most
- Can't sit still for long periods of time
- Uses action words

The first reason I gave you, such an extensive list of traits, is because now it is going to be easier to recognize the traits of those people you come in contact with daily. Having this knowledge will allow you to understand that person better and know their personal representation of the world. Second is to use it to achieve rapport using their specific modality, for instance, if you are car salesmen, here are three different ways to get the same message across to Auditory, Visual and Kinesthetic types:

Visual: Come and **look** at the **styling** of this car, the **sleek lines** and **design** of this car are second to none. Have you **seen** the interior of the car with **exquisite leather seats** and how the **dashboard lights up**?

Auditory: It **sounds** like you are ready to purchase a car. This car runs so smooth that you cannot even **hear** a hum from the outside of the car. It is just that **quiet**.

Kinesthetic: Speaking **slowing touching them on the shoulder** pointing in the direction of the car saying "I had a **feeling** that was the car you were interested in. You will just **love** the upgraded stereo system. Can you **imagine gripping** on to the steering wheel while the car **hugs** the road going 60mph? Come check out the interior and **feel the texture** of your seats. How are you going to **feel** driving your new car home tonight?

The best way to get better at rapport is to practice the skills on an ongoing basis.

Enhancing Rapport Skills

When speaking to friends, family or co-workers, pick out one specific to match or mirror. Pick one trait per day and practice it until it becomes second-nature. Within a short time, you'll have an entire tool belt of rapport skills to choose from. Most importantly, have fun! You will acquire insight utilizing these tools, and they can only strengthen your relationships, both new and old.

Written by Suzan Gole: Transform Your Senses ◊
www.transformyoursenses.com
suzan@transformyoursenses.com

Our Mission Statement: We are dedicated and intensely interested in enriching the lives of others. We do this through using proven Whole-Mind tools to empower you in your life. We know through creative interaction and deep listening, we can help you expand all of your senses allowing you to move toward positive change while opening your awareness to all of the possibilities you've ever envisioned and make abundance in your life a reality!

CHAPTER FIVE

Getting from No to Yes
by Reverend Jeanne Munsell

Remember back to when you were a small child and the adult in your life wanted you to entertain yourself? Often, my adults would give me one or two doll like figures (stuffed toy, action figure, dolls, etc.). The goal was for me to go into my private world of having total power and have the dolls "play" with me. I always interpreted that as permission to have the dolls do exactly what I want them to do. I would tell the first doll to hold the second doll's hand… and voilà! It immediately would occur. I would then tell the second doll to run away and POOF! The second doll would run away. Why is it that, as a small child, I had absolute control over my dolls?

Of course, I got total compliance because I controlled the dolls completely. So why is it today that, as an adult, it appears as if I do not have as much control in my own personal universe or in my sphere of influence?

The answer lies in how stuck or unstuck I am with the flexibility of how I relate to myself and others.

Why are people so stubborn? What I am saying is important for them.

People, including the person you refer to as "stubborn," are that way when they do not feel heard, appreciated, or liked. You tend to get stuck in the box of your own problem (a real problem, advice needed, when buying or selling something, or staying on a path you have chosen).

So how do I get someone to feel like they like me? Do they have to REALLY like me? Yes and No.

You need to have credibility with the one you are talking with. In other words, if they see you as someone who just blows a bunch of smoke, all the time, the likelihood of having a positive influence on someone (yes, even yourself) is lessened.

How do I change that? Like in the previous and following chapters, living your life with integrity and excellence. In addition to the foundation of living in integrity and excellence, there are a few other things you can do.

First of all, people like others who are like them and who they perceive like them as they are.

What does that mean for me? It means that if you gain rapport with someone, you will imitate what they are doing for a while, and then you will test to see if you have gained rapport by seeing if they imitate you in something small you do. For example, you may want to sit with the same posture as the other; you may want to speak in the same sentence structure they speak in. If they speak fast, you speak as fast, if they speak slowly; you speak at the same pace. If they scratch their nose, you scratch your nose, etc. If you have imitated them well, when you make a small, but different behavior, they will follow. This is called rapport. Rapport is the unconscious belief that someone is like them.

Why should I do this? People like people who are like themselves and who they perceive like them. Remember the old story—often circulated around the Holidays—"He with the most toys wins?" While that story may not be true, what is true is that "She with the most flexibility in her behavior wins!"

How do I see things differently?

Seeing the problem differently than the other person is the key to helping them resolve their issue.

Often a simple re-frame will help them over the barrier wall of the "problem". A re-frame (which is learned well in my NLP classes) is simply putting the positive attributes of the "problem" into a different context that shows off the strength of the "problem" behaviors.

For example, a first glance, this helicopter could look as if it were crashing.

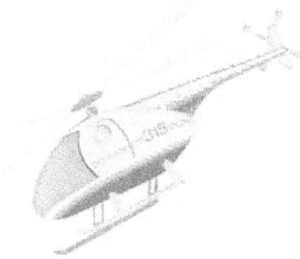

However, on further review of this helicopter's situation, you see that the helicopter is sweeping down on this home...

to drop water on the fire that's burning in the home.

This is a reframe. It puts what they perceived as a problem into a different context that makes what we saw, heard, felt and thought different.

A parent once came to renowned Psychiatrist and Hypnotherapist Milton Erickson with the following problem with his teen-aged child.

"This girl is totally stubborn and rebellious. She will not do anything I tell her to without knowing all the reasons and evidence as to why she should do it" complained the parent to Erickson in front of the teen.

Erickson thought a moment—he realized that the teen was going through a natural developmental phase. Erickson's response was, "And how proud you will be when she says NO to her peers and is able to stand up for herself and take care of herself because your child is so strong."

This simple re-frame allowed the parent to see the child's behavior not as rebellion, but as building up her strength to say NO to things that are not in her best interest and allowing her to fully care for herself due to her strong mind.

Values? Why would I care? Right is right, right?

Another way of helping others and yourself is to know their values.

What is a value? It is what motivates us to do what we do and to know if we did it well or not.

So why are values important?

If you know a person's values (or your own) you can speak to their values in the way you present something so that they resonate with what it is you are presenting, and it becomes the default choice regarding what to do.

If I know that the person I am talking with is wanting to become thin and svelte, however, the person has a value that thin and svelte persons are sexually promiscuous (which to them is against their highest value of sexual purity), no matter how much I tell them to put down that 3,000 calorie pizza, they probably will not be successful in keeping the weight off, if it ever comes off.

Why? The person does NOT want to be sexually promiscuous. They may agree that getting off the extra weight will help them be healthier, more attractive, etc. However, by NOT addressing their primary value—"I don't want to be sexually promiscuous," I will not help them get and keep the weight off. If, however, I address how having the strength to put down the pizza means you will have all the strength and power you need to stay sexually pure, it is more likely that the person will accept becoming svelte and thin and want to work towards the proof that they have the power to be sexually pure. This is why most weight reduction programs fail. They only focus on the calories and not what the calories, the weight, or the result of thin and svelte means.

The Virtual Lap Band works so much better, because these issues are addressed and the weight comes off as effectively as Lap Band surgery. The difference is that the Virtual Lap Band helps a person keep the new thin, healthy, svelte lifestyle for all the person's values have been discussed. Blockages have been dissolved and the person is totally motivated to be the new person they now are.

It works the same in sales and persuasion. If I want you to buy my pitch (be it: buy this car, phone, or goods -- as well as adopt a concept that is healthier for them), I simply ask them,

"What is important about_____?" (What exactly do I want to persuade them into adopting or purchasing from me?)

I ask this question a few times in different ways.

Then, I give their values back to them in the order of what THEY see as most important. (Remember NLP is all about influencing the one who will make the change.)

For example, I want my eight year old child to go to bed early. I am tired, exhausted and I need him to go to bed early. My first step is to ask my child what he likes about the time he goes to bed. Being a typical eight year old, he replies,

"Big people stay up late."

What else is important to you about what time you go to bed?

"I have to watch my favorite superhero show."

That's wonderful—"What else tells you what is important about when you go to bed?"

"I get to be in control."

I have just found out what is most important to my child about when he goes to bed. He is in control, he is modeling what big people do (adults), and he gets to watch his favorite show.

So I look at the TV schedule and see that one of his favorite superhero programs is on at 7:30 tonight.

I say to my son, "That is wonderful. How would you like to be in charge of your bed time tonight, just like me?" (It should get a resounding YES!). "Great!" Would you like to go to bed before or after your favorite superhero show is on tonight? (He can only answer before or after—no other answer is correct). He will say, "After" (After is being up later, in control and allows him to watch is favorite show, just like adults). "Great", I tell him. "Let's get your bath and get you all ready for bed NOW, so that you can watch your show and not be disturbed. Then you will go directly to bed. Sound good?"

Since I met all his top values for when he goes to bed, he willingly does as asked so that he can be in control, be like an adult and watch his show.

Learning more about values, is one of the things I teach in my class called <u>Selling Ice Cubes on the Tundra</u>. If you can sell an ice cube where it is so cold that everything remains frozen nearly all year long, you can sell anything, anywhere, at anytime.

OK, I've got that. So, how do I communicate with NLP?

Simple. NLP is designed to allow you to make the most impact, the quickest, and for the most long-lasting changes using things we do every day, with a purpose. So, by following the few suggestions given in this book, you will motivate yourself and others (if you choose) to be un-stuck in thinking up ways of expressing yourself, of being motivated, and having behaviors consistent with what you really want.

It is always best to persuade yourself to be totally aligned with what you want before you persuade others to get in alignment with you. (You want them to model your excellence, your integrity, your motivation.)

How do I inspire others and myself with NLP?

For a simple re-cap, I start with myself focusing on what I want and aligning my conscious and unconscious minds so that I make my own changes easily and effectively. I am in control of how I feel, and I use the tools provided to keep me in the mindset I choose. Being at the mercy of what others say and do is a state that is too stuck and not me anymore. I choose to have control over what I feel, say, think, hear and enjoy. If I need to get angry, or vent another emotion that does not bring me health, happiness or productivity, I choose when and where to experience that emotion—it does not control me.

I make sure that I live with integrity and excellence. Perfection is a myth and an energy drainer—so I let go of perfection for excellence.

I gain rapport with all so that I am liked and like the one I would like to influence.

I have the most flexibility in how I communicate, so I win.

I understand my personal values and others as well. I speak to the values to create the most change and the most resonance with the person I am motivating.

I use my ability to think outside of the box the "problem" is in, and I reframe the "problem" into a different context so that the problem is now an asset.

How do I move myself from stuck to having choices and acting on them?

Usually when you are stuck it means that you are either striving for perfection (which is a myth and not obtainable), OR you have allowed what others and you perceive as 'your problem' to not have any solutions. The truth is, all challenges have solutions. The solution may not be exactly what you are looking for at this point, but there is a solution.

I am often touched by what some inspirational authors have said. One that I heard lately said that God (or the Universe or Science or your higher power) already knew you would come up against this challenge. And perhaps the challenge was permitted to be there in order for you to grow, or to get you to see and act on other options that are available, but for the moment you have dismissed them.

Challenges are there for a purpose—for you to learn something and continue on with your growth. Simply put, Challenges are what future motivation is made up of.

To stay un-stuck and motivated, I suggest you continue to grow and pursue how you can best keep yourself motivated, on track and doing what you have always dreamed of doing. If this means that you read more books, go to seminars and trainings, you do what you need to do to keep growing and being excellent.

My goal is for others to see me as their "go-to" person and I am happy that I not only help myself daily, but I am able to help others in conversation or with a few techniques. How about you?

So how fun is that!!! Isn't it great to be in control?

It is great to know that I have the ability to persuade people to do good things and to motivate them. I also have the power within me, by taking every thought captive and thinking only on those things which bring happiness, joy, health, goodness, etc. and by using the powerful truths found in this book to keep me in a happy, productive state. I choose who and what I allow to influence me as well as who and what I choose to influence.

Life is good—living motivated and un-stuck.

Reverend Jeanne Munsell, D.D., M.A. LMFT was born in Florida and grew up in a regular blue-collar home. At a very young age, Jeanne decided she wanted to help others as well as earn the right to help others. Dr. Jeanne is an Internationally Board Certified Hypnotherapist, NLP Master Practitioner and Trainer, Licensed Marriage and Family Therapist (27391 CA). She holds a Doctorate, two Master's Degrees (Theologically-based and Psychologically-based) as well as a teaching Degree (B.S. from Florida State University)

"I am a Certified Trainer (also a Master Practitioner and Practitioner) of:

- NLP
- Hypnosis (Krasner, Elman, Erickson, Group, Stage, Children, Rapid Inductions)
- CORE coaching,
- TIME Techniques
- Ho 'Oponono (Forgiveness techniques)
- EFT

I know a little about needing to make changes, not wanting to change (being stuck) and being totally surprised at how easy it is to change. I have used these tools in my own life to donate over 160 excessive pounds of body weight back to the world, overcome health challenges, improve my memory, rid myself of learning disabilities, and forgive others in a real way. Once plagued by diabetes, high blood pressure, kidney disease, and vision problems, I am now totally symptom-free to the point that my new doctors have asked me to verify I once had such diagnosis/need for treatment. I began to study and apply hypnosis and NLP in my own life, and I've gotten such phenomenal results that I just have to share them with you. These are resourceful secrets that have been used since Biblical times."

"I specialize in the virtual lap band. This has the same success rate as bariatric surgery, without the complications of surgery. The best thing about the virtual lap band is that no work needs to be missed, no one has to pick you up from the hospital, and more people keep their new, healthier body than those who underwent the surgery. Whatever you want to do, I will easily and effectively help you—usually in one session."

Visit my website at www.AbundanTransformation.com or call me at 1 (888) 832-3261 for a free evaluation.

I make Dreams come True.

CHAPTER SIX

Chunking for Success
by Cathy Meyers

Up and down the mountain (of thoughts)

For the New Year, I took a short getaway vacation (in Palm Springs). I took a hike up the mountain. From the top, I could see not only my hotel, but surrounding things, then the whole city, roads to other places and another city and the whole valley. As I looked over the whole scene I thought about what I could do with my life that would have a more far reaching effect than just me.

I came up with various visions and ideas that could improve many lives, not just mine. My intension was to make a difference in a time when many people need a change for the positive. I wrote out these inspiring ideas with a passion and energy. I wrote with a real sense of excitement that I could contribute something worthwhile. As I wrote, more ideas came to me as one sprang from another. It was an "enlightening" experience.

As I started the journey back down to my room, I though "Okay, all these ideas are great but how can I make this happen... where do I start? It was an interesting experience as I walked down, getting more and more into the specific detail on how I would implement my ideas. When I returned to my hotel room, I started to organize my ideas on sticky notes getting down to the specific details of where I could start and how to implement my ideas.

Two types of people

Have you ever noticed how some people seem to live their lives on a mountain top? They are the visionary types, full of ideas, some with broad applications. Then, there are others who look past what is in front of them into the details and specifics.

I like to refer to these ways of thinking as "chunking." When you are thinking of the big picture you are "chunking up." When you are getting into details and being specific you are "chunking down."

Advantages to both – Chunking up and down

At this time in history a person could make a very good income from one really good idea. However, without the details and a specific plan of action the idea might not get off the ground. Visionary people are great at running an organization or company. and, they do better when they delegate the details to someone else who has a gift for that.

Now it's true that if you are a "chunked up" visionary person you could get impatient with someone who wants to know all the details, or how are you going to do what you're talking about. A "chunked down" person might not see any practical application to your big ideas. You might even interpret that as "raining on your parade". The trick is not to take it personal and simply realize that the person thinks in a different chunk size that you do.

On the other hand, if you are a detailed, chunked down person, a visionary person might become bored as you discuss the details of a project. They might not see the value of your attention to detail. Once again, it's nothing personal. They are looking at things from a mountain top level and you are looking at things from the hotel room level.

Both points of view are extremely valuable.

Chunking for motivation and overcoming overwhelm

Have you ever become bored or disinterested in a project? Whether you are just getting started or are already in the middle of it, then chunking up is the thing to do. Chances are you have gotten bogged down or stuck in the details. Chunk up to the big picture… the purpose of why you are doing it in the first place. What will getting this accomplished allow you to do, or do for you? Keep asking yourself questions until you find your motivation… until you get excited and enthusiastic about your purpose and the real reason behind what you're doing. You will most likely end up connecting with one of your most important values in some way.

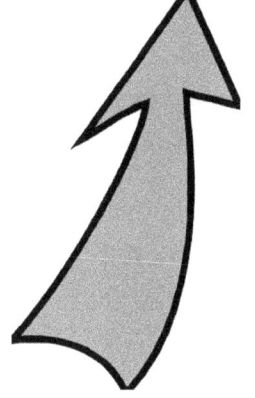

What if you're overwhelmed? Simply chunk down the project into its parts; you can break it down by using a timeline and make a note of any due dates or deadlines. Another possibility is dividing the task into sections that you can delegate to others or to different groups. Then do a timeline for each section. The goal is to get to at least one action step that you can do today or right now. Chunking down can also help you make sure you are being realistic.

Chunking for groups and teams

The same method can be used for group and team motivation. Get the whole group on board by chunking high enough to get agreement. When everyone is in agreement on the big picture or the purpose of the group or activity, then the details don't seem to be such a sticking point. Then, to get started, chunk down to details.

You can assign tasks according to each person's chunking style, which helps everyone be more productive.

When working with a team or board that is negotiating with another team or board, chunk your side up to a common agreement first, so you are all together before meeting with the other side. If your team gets split at some point, take a break or schedule another session until you can come together on what's really important.

Doing this exercise is also helpful for resolving conflicts within your life. Chunk your conflicted "parts" up to what's most important. You may find that you are in agreement after all.

Chunking helps you communicate and connect

After listening to someone speak, usually for a short time, you can get an idea of what level of chunking they are thinking about, all the way from big picture (chunked up) or specific details (chunked down) or somewhere in-between. Being aware and noticing someone's "chunk size" can help you communicate by matching and speaking to them on the same level. This will help you to connect with people from their point of view. After you have connected with them where they're at and have some rapport, try this little exercise. Chunk them up by asking questions about what is really important to them.

You can also chunk them down by asking for details on how they would implement their plan. By doing this, you can really get to know a person and maybe even help them get clear on some things for themselves.

Chunking for Productive Meetings

Before: Start with stating for yourself what positive outcomes you would like pursuant to the meeting. Chunk up to the big picture. Why are you having the meeting in the first place? Make sure you're focused on the Positive aspects - the things that you want, not any Negative aspects - the things you don't want. This will be useful for keeping you and everyone else focused on the goal.

Then, chunk down to your "evidence procedure". What that means is to take note of what will need to happen (your evidence) for you to **know** that you got the outcomes that you were aiming for. Be specific about how to tell that you reached the goal or outcome.

During. Remembering that both points of view are important, validate someone's suggestion before you counter it with something different.

Handling disagreement: When having trouble getting everyone on the same page, chunk the group up together to the big picture about what the group wants to accomplish. Ask, why are we here in the first place? When you get everyone to agree on a common point, it is easier to then chunk down to the details of how it is going to be accomplished. When someone gets bogged down in a detail, remind them of the big picture.

When making a proposal:

First: State your reason. Give only 1 or 2 focused reasons (big picture). Giving more reasons gives more opportunity for disagreement. The weakest one will most likely get picked.

Second: Give the explanation

Third: Present the proposal (Not the other way around)

Chunking for salespeople

For example, when showing homes as a real estate agent, when clients get bogged down in the details of what they want in the home or spouses don't agree, chunk them up to what's really important – the big picture.

What can I learn from this?

1) Appreciate other points of view that are different from how you see it. It helps if you can see things as just "different" instead of right or wrong. It helps to validate/appreciate someone's point of view before you give them yours.

2) Both styles of thinking are valuable. We need each other.

3) Recognizing chunking style helps you connect with people on their level. Learn to be flexible in your conversation.

4) Help you look for win/win situations and avoid looking at things as right or wrong.

Cathy Meyers is a Master Practitioner and Trainer of NLP and Time Line Therapy(tm), as well as a certified master hypnotherapist and master success coach. She is an expert in getting unstuck by combining these tools with Christian beliefs and values.

She is co-owner of The NLP Solution at www.TheNLPSolution.com. Contact her at cathymycoach@gmail.com

CHAPTER SEVEN

Turn on Your Personal Television!

by Val Rensink

What would be your Personal TV System?
Take a moment and design with me!

How does sound affect motivation?

Let me share what my Personal TV System would be. Just off the top of my head, I would have to start with the sound. It would be a Bose Sound system. Can you hear how good this will sound? Very small black speakers, just little cubes placed around the room for stereo, surround, directional, and delayed sound. There would be a huge bass speaker. I think I would put it in back of the room. This Bose would be able to reproduce all the sounds that you hear in normal life and more. It would have the ability to make those fine distinctions of whisper and pin drop. It would reproduce the full range of sound from deep ocean rumblings to piercingly shrill sea gull cries.

If there are two voices speaking… it could separate sound like two conversations, one on each side of the room. What awesome sound it produces. From this sound system, the theme from 2001 Space Odyssey hits all its chilling and amazing notes. From this sound system, Yellowstone's distant thunder storms rumble the air and shake the ground. From this sound system, the sound of corn silk growing could be heard and would invite me in close to the experience.

The design of the Bose would allow my Ears to be the final judge. Is the bass too booming? Back it off just right. There would be pitch reproduction without slow, muddy, thick, fat, loose bass. It would be quick, clean, tight and precise. Oh wow! I can hear the attack and delay of a rock band's drum.

Midrange feels hollow or boxy? Fill it in. Ear Perfect! This sound has the energy in it. It would be sweet, smooth like velvet. The Midrange is your transparent audio heart. Treble to Tinny? Make it expand as though the sound of the treble were lifting you above. The Bose would allow me to place the sound chest centered or like the distant rumbling of a train. I feel it approach and then it's passing. You might say the sound would be so good that I could feel the swoosh of the train resonating inside of me. Oh, it would be a great sound system, one that I could change and create.

Are you with me? Can you hear the sounds? Trust your ears.

I think you get the idea of how important sound is to me. Maybe sound is very important to you. Maybe you are more interested in the picture. So let's look at that.

How do pictures affect motivation?

Next, imagine with me a high definition plasma 60 inch screen. (You can decide: Sony, LG or whatever is best). So the screen would reproduce every color you can imagine. It can reproduce all spectrums of light intensity. The screen would allow me to see one picture. For more diversity, it would allow me to put a picture within a picture. I could see two similar or two different pictures at the same time. I could choose which picture would be up front and central.

Can you feel my excitement go up? I can. I could have one picture that I am watching and another on something that really interests me just in the corner. No, I am not double tasking. I am going with where my interest is most drawn. Yes, I could hook up my blue ray DVD or my Playstation gaming console. Oh my gosh, this is so much fun. I can play the *kind of pictures* that I want and I can play them *when I want.* My personal Television Screen is awesome.

Now, let's look at a very low tech aspect of the screen. The Lowly Mounting Bracket! The mounting bracket lets me point it where I will. It is a movable bracket with a telescoping feature. I can bring the screen in close to me or put it back up against the wall. Do I want it on the floor? There it goes. Do I want it on the ceiling? There it goes. (Yes, even basic things like a lowly mounting bracket are in my control.) Now let's move up to a higher tech item: the world's best remote control.

The remote control is simply the world's best. It has large, well-sculpted buttons. It has sleek, modern ergonomics. It has one-touch magic for picture correction. This remote control even has a self-finding system so you can never lose it! (Although I am talking to you about the ability to control the screen, you can get a feeling for this remote, right?) Holding the remote reminds me of that old TV show Outer Limits. Do you recall the opening part of the monologue and what it used to say?

"There is nothing wrong with your television set. Do not attempt to adjust the picture. We are controlling transmission. We will control the horizontal. We will control the vertical. We can change the focus to a soft blur, or sharpen it to crystal clarity. Sit quietly, and for the next hour we will control all that you see and hear."

Well, let me repeat, there is nothing wrong with your TV. You will be controlling the transmission. You will control the horizontal. You will control the vertical. I would sit up, be engaged and adjust the controls the way I wanted. I could take my remote and adjust the picture so that it produced the most incredible tones, hues, colors and brightness that I liked. I would control the horizontal and the vertical. I could make the colors vibrate like silver bells ringing or bronze bells clanging. The colors would laugh, and dance and lament. The colors would have soul and passion and life and death. The reds would run blood red and the blues ocean blue.

Yes, on some of the pictures, like a candlelight meal or a night walk by an ocean shore through woods at Pfeiffer Big Sur, I would want the lighting subdued. I would soften it to a gentle bluish hue. You know what I mean. It would create a certain feeling of closeness or intimacy. On other pictures, like one of football or other action sports, lights on and up, not so much that they wash the picture out. I would adjust the contrast and sharpen the picture so that the scrimmage is bright and clear.

So, I think you get an idea of how important the picture is to me. I suppose the picture could be just as important to you. Perhaps for a moment you are realizing how many things go into making an amazing picture. And maybe just now you are realizing that the picture (and the sounds) helps to produce feeling. And feelings are really important.

Let's put a handle on our next experience of turning your Personal Television on. Now, perhaps you would have started with how you feel when you are engaged in TV.

How does feeling affect motivation?

Let's get a grip on this one. The particular sound and the particular picture of my Personal TV are there to produce a certain feeling. If I am watching Mel Gibson in Braveheart with my son, I want the battle scenes to pull us into that excitement and danger. I want my heart to speed up and my attention to be riveted. When I watch Louisa May Alcott's Little Women with my daughter, I want us to feel the poverty of Meg, Jo, Beth and

Amy as they sit in their living room lamenting, and although feeling a sad sympathy is not my favorite feeling, it is appropriate to the sounds and pictures before us.

A favorite scene of mine from Star Wars (because it is both action and romance) is when Princess Leia kisses Luke Skywalker just before escaping the imperial guards by swinging across the chasm.

Now, I realize that I can up my feelings when I turn my own personal Television on. I would bring in a DBox Motion Code. If you haven't had the chance to do this, let me share with you how much this adds to the feeling experience. The very chair you are sitting in responds to all the Sounds and Pictures you are hearing and seeing. Did the action in the picture bring you up to the edge of a hill and down? Your chair intensifies that visual by going up and down. This is something like a tourist on the Disneyland ride "Star Tours". This DBox Motion Code helps to take you literally inside the picture. This movement system helps to reinforce your experience of the pictures and the sounds you are seeing and hearing. This is unique as it immerses you in a realistic experience.

I know that all of this is edging its way on to a virtual reality. Think of the movies Lawnmower Man or more recently in Tron Legacy which has aspects of virtual reality in them. You are not watching the action you are in the action.

So, when you <u>Turn Your Personal Television On</u>!, you are immersed and increasing an experience in Sounds, Sights and Feeling that fit you to a T.

So how does this affect motivation?

So, what does this all have to do with motivation? How could this help you in keeping yourself motivated? Would you like to be able to control your personal motivation?

Now you can. You have pictures, sounds and feeling inside of you already.

I would like you to take a picture that you have of something pleasant that has happened to you. Please take something small. Maybe you have been to Disneyland and can recall a pleasant time there. Alternatively, maybe you have been to a favorite place on a certain day that turned out just right. In your mind's eye, go to that place right now. Just float back right now and float down inside your body and see what you saw and hear what you heard and feel the feelings you felt.

(As you do this exercise, and please do it, if you have to pause or open your eyes during the exercise, that is okay. Take that pause and then close your eyes and return to where you are, now.)

Now let us focus on a few important things.

What sounds are important to you? Is it the voice of someone special? Is it the sound of the music? Are there background sounds that really add to that certain day? As best you can recall, hear those sounds now.

Picture that certain day. What was the weather like? Were you inside or outside? What was around you? Who was with you? What were the colors like? Bring all of that back right now. Recall the sights and the sounds of that certain day. What feelings does that bring? Does it bring back memories to you a certain happiness, calmness, excitement or what? What is the feeling of that certain day? *Now turn your own Personal Television on.*

First, I want you to adjust the picture. Make it brighter. Really brighten it up, but don't wash it out.

Now check on your feelings. Does that make you feel better? Adjust that picture so that it makes you feel the best it can. Adjust the clarity. Feel Better? Adjust the richness of the colors. Feel Better? Get the picture of that certain day so that if it were food you would be licking your lips. (Yes. Just like some Madison Avenue advertiser). Is the picture a still snapshot? Make it move and see what that does to your feelings. Is the picture Panoramic? Then put a frame around it. If it is framed, experiment with having it panoramic. See which way makes it feel more alive and vibrant. Then, hold it there.

Second, I want you to adjust the sounds in your picture. On the certain day, take the sounds and make them louder. Does that feel better? Alternatively, make them softer. Does that feel better? Move the sound out away from you. Does that make it feel better? Slow the sound down. Does that make it feel better? I think you have the idea. Make the sound, adjust the sound and let your ear be the judge. Make the sound hearing perfect so that it creates the best feelings inside of you.

Third, and finally, I want you to adjust the feeling. Oh there is so much to feelings. Adjust how you feel inside your body. Adjust how you feel about feeling really good on this day. Adjust how you feel the temperature, the breeze, the sun on your face. Adjust and ask "Does that make it feel better?"

As a side note, if there was something you ate, and it tasted good, up the taste and ask "Does that make it feel better?" If there was the smell of flowers or pine trees or something that you liked, up the fragrance of that item and ask yourself, "Does that make it feel better?" (If you have ever been on the ride from California Adventure/Disneyland called Soarin' over California you will know the importance of Fragrance. Fragrance from Orange trees, Pine trees and Ocean Salt Air enhances the ride.)

Now, once you have this all, lock it in. (I like to think of sound of a Mercedes Benz door closing to lock it in.) You have the Picture, Sound, and Feeling of the picture. You have the Taste and Smell of the picture. You have it all! Now ask yourself, now that you have made it the best, "Does this motivate you?" The answer should be a yes and must be a yes if you actually did the process as described. Remember, the first time is practice and the second time will get it done for you.

Bonus Section
Turn Your Personal Television On! Motivate Yourself to Success.

I didn't promise you a bonus, but you get one anyway. How would you like to take the feeling of motivation and use it to make you successful? And more importantly, successful at something you haven't done yet?

Here is how to do that. First, take that motivating picture with all the sights, sounds, feelings, tastes, and smells that are just right. Make sure you have it locked in. Now, pull up the picture of something that doesn't create that feeling of motivation. Maybe you are facing something, and it creates in you a feeling of uncertainty.

Now, this is really important. I want you to notice one or two things that are different between the pictures. Let me suggest that you notice if the picture is still in the less motivating one (and the picture is moving in the motivating one). That would be really good. Or, let me suggest that you notice the difference between where the picture is located. (Let us say that the less motivating picture is far away and the motivating picture is up close. That is a good difference.) So, what now?? Let us say that the best difference between the two pictures is the motion and still difference. Let us say that your motivating picture is moving and your less motivating picture is still.

Listen closely, I want you to pull up your less motivating picture – the still one – and I want you to make it move. And, once you have it moving, I want you to lock it in.

Then, just take a moment. Clear your mind; look out the window. Get up and walk around, if you like. And when you sit down ask yourself "How do I feel about that less motivating picture?" My prediction is you will feel very motivated. You will have a motivation for success. (By the way, this works one hundred percent of the time.)

Well, thank you for reading my chapter, and our book. I appreciate your comments and questions.

Val Rensink Is a Trainer and Personal Coach. he works in groups or one-on-one. he has experience in the Sales with Real estate and Auto Sales. his motto is, "I specialize in results."

Certified Trainer in NLP Certified Trainer in Hypnosis Practitioner in TimeLine TechniquesTM Practitioner in Success Coaching Licensed Broker Realtor

Val is co-owner of The NLP Solution at www.TheNLPSolution.com. To Contact Val, email him at: ValMyCoach@gmail.com

*   When we get to the bottom line, motivation is a feeling. So, the sounds and sights we experience, recall and create help to shape the feelings of motivation.

CHAPTER EIGHT

States and Anchors
by Ronald Berg

How would you like it if I were to show you a way to change your emotional state at will? Would you want to be shown how and taught the tools so that you could have confidence, happiness, resourcefulness or any other positive emotional state instantly and at will? Would that be of value to you? Of course it would.

Many people think of their emotional state as a type of noun. In other words, they are a thing that you have or catch or have to deal with, rather than a feeling we get, that changes depending on our response to the world around us. This limiting belief takes away our control over our own emotions. Have you ever heard some say that they suffer from depression? What they did was make that state of depressed feelings and turn it into something we would call a "pseudo noun."

Since you cannot put depression into a wheelbarrow or any other container, it has no physical form at all. It, by definition, isn't a noun. Even someone suffering from feelings of sadness can help themselves by eliminating this limiting belief. Emotional states are also not goals. Ever heard anyone say that they want to be happier in the New Year or future? This is taking an emotional state and trying to make it into a goal, but a goal is something that has steps and takes time while a state can be had instantly.

You can instantly change your state. If I were to ask you to think of a happy memory from your past, a specific happy memory when you were on an amazing vacation or something really great happened. Imagine yourself floating back to that moment, seeing everything you saw, hearing everything you had heard and feeling everything you felt. Really feel that happiness inside. If, right now you don't have those feelings of happiness inside, you did the exercise wrong. Do it again, and this time experience those feelings.

Congratulations, just by doing that, your state has changed, and it happened instantly. The choice of how long that change of your emotional state lasts is up to you. There were no steps that you had to take or obstacles that had to be overcome, all you had to do was think of it, and it was yours. Goals need to have steps and there are always obstacles that need to be overcome to attain it.

The reason there has to be obstacles is that if there were none, you would already have it. A goal is also measurable while a state is infinite or not measurable. How do you measure more happiness? You can't, but you can measure a goal.

Understanding this is extremely important as we move on to talk about anchors and ways to install in ourselves the tools and resources to change our state instantly and at will.

When I was growing up, the only thing I thought of when I heard the word anchor was dropping a steel hook in the mud at the bottom of a lake to hold our boat secure and in one place. While learning NLP, I learned a new meaning of the word. Anchoring in NLP is based on the experiments that a scientist named Pavlov did with his dog.

What happened was that Pavlov noticed that his dog would salivate when he would see his food coming. What this means is that the dog was preparing for the meal, even before he started eating, at the unconscious level. The saliva increasing is part of normal digestion and happens when the food is in our mouth. The revelation was that the body can start the digestion just by seeing food.

The next and logical question was to ask if an unconscious process like digestion could be caused to happen without any food at all, by linking food to an external trigger. In this case, a bell that Pavlov would ring. So Pavlov started ringing a bell at meal time when showing the dog the food. After doing this at every meal, the dog got to the point that all Pavlov had to do was ring the bell without any food around and the dog would start to salivate. What he did was anchor the sound of the bell at the unconscious level to food. So the dog would unconsciously prepare for food with the bell in exactly the same way that he would prepare for food when actually seeing it. In the world of therapy this is called "behavioral psychology," or the study of what affects our behavior.

The interesting thing is that at one time it was believed that people, being far more complex than dogs, would not respond as easily to this kind of programming. The reality is actually the exact opposite. People are far more complex, and because of that complexity, we respond even faster and more easily to this kind of programming. In fact, we do it all the time.

When I was younger I grew up in Lake Tahoe, a beautiful area that is still just as amazing today as it was when I was a kid. One of the biggest landmarks in my hometown was a tree in the middle of the road in the center of town. It was a giant pine tree that you could see as soon as you started coming into town. I still go up there from time to time and whenever I would come into town, I would see the tree and immediately be flooded with pleasant feelings of peace, contentment and all the other positive feelings of being home. I had unknowingly anchored those feeling to that tree.

A few years back, the tree was cut down. Ever since then, those amazing feelings of peace I would get as soon as I came into town vanished. The positive anchor that I associated home with was removed. I still love the town and enjoy visiting, but all those feelings I enjoyed every time I came into town are just gone. In the world of NLP, we would say that someone collapsed my anchor. In other words, they eliminated it. While that was a very strong positive anchor, we can have negative anchors as well.

Negative anchors often happen accidentally. A perfect example of an accidental negative anchor is when a mother picks up and holds her child every time they get hurt. It is a natural thing to do, but if that is the main time that hugs take place, then those feelings of pain and hurt and discomfort can get accidentally anchored to the hug from that person. For kids, what they start to feel is uncomfortable with hugging their mom, often pulling away from the hug reflexively to prevent those feelings.

I have personally seen a child pull away from one parent trying to hug them and run to the other for comfort. The one they run to is the one that has not, unknowingly, set up their hug as a negative anchor. Does this mean that I think kids should not receive comfort when they are sick or hurt? Certainly not! But care must be taken to consciously keep the hug set up as a positive anchor.

The way to prevent the negative anchor from being attached to the hug is to make sure that you hug the kid more for positive reasons such as praising the kid for something they accomplished, happy events and just to show them that you love them, far more often than you do for negative ones like when they get hurt or are sick, and you want to comfort them. This way you are actually doing an even better job of comforting them. Having set up the hug as a powerful positive anchor, it will feel better and more comforting to the child when you give that comfort hug.

The anchor is not firmly in place on the first event. It is the repeated events that get the anchor in place. You have probably noticed that when your spouse just looks at you a certain way, and you immediately get upset. Nothing has been said yet, but they have "pushed your buttons." This is a perfect example of an anchor that was established over time.

The first time they looked at you that way it probable had no negative effect at all. The second time you got the look, your unconscious referenced back to the first time and added that to the response. This continued until the anchor was firmly in place and just looking at you with that expression is enough to trigger the negative emotions.

It is possible to have an anchor placed on one event, but the emotions to set it have to be very powerful. A phobia would be an example of an extreme negative anchor. Take the child who experiences a near drowning experience. The extremely powerful emotions of fear and anxiety became immediately fixed to water to the point they have severe anxiety and fear anytime they come near water. There are cases of people who had some traumatic experience and now, whenever they are in a similar setting, have an immediate phobia response. Some have gone through years of therapy to get the phobia under control. At the conscious level, they may understand everything about why they react the way they do, yet every time they are in that situation, the phobia comes up. Why?

Well, because the problem is not a conscious problem. They do not decide that there is a pool over there so they need to start going into a panic attack. It happens at the unconscious level, so the conscious therapy fails to deal with it. This is simply because you can't fix an unconscious problem at the conscious level; you have to fix it at the unconscious level.

I am sure that you have, at some point in your life, experienced an emotion that was brought on by a place or smell. What this proves is that you have the ability to change your emotional state instantly. If just a smell or sight can trigger an emotional change, then you can have control over your emotions. The "buttons" you have that bring on negative emotions can be altered or eliminated entirely by collapsing them. In the case of positive emotions, you can set up resource anchors to install the emotional states that you want. One of the most useful resource anchors available is the ring of power.

A ring of power is a resource anchor that you set up with all the resources you need to be empowered. This is a virtual ring, not an actual ring. You do not want or need a circle that is physically on the ground to put the power in because you want to take that ring with you so that you can use it anywhere. The technique is easy to do an incredibly powerful. To do it, we just go through some very easy steps. The first step is to imagine a ring of power on the ground in front of you. While standing, imagine that ring of power just waiting to be charged up with all the tools you need to be completely empowered.

The next step is to recall a memory in which you experienced a positive empowering state. We will do several different ones to really charge up the ring.

So ask yourself, can you recall a past event in which you felt resourceful? One where you knew you had all the tools to accomplish your goals? Can you recall a specific event? Great. Imagine yourself going back to that exact moment where you felt the state of resourcefulness. Float down into your body, seeing what you saw, hearing what you heard and feel all the feelings of being incredibly resourceful. When you feel those emotions begin to peak, imagine that powerful resource filling into your chest and coming down your arms. Direct that resource to pour into the ring of power in front of you.

Allow all of it to drain out of your arms and into the ring. Next, can you recall another event in which you felt resourceful? The more events that represent the state you want, the more powerful the ring of power becomes. This is truly one case where more is better. After going through two or more events that you had that state in and charging the ring with them, move on to other states to empower you.

For every state that you use, think of a past event in which you had that state. Make it a specific event; generalized ones do not get the same intensities that specific ones do. Imagine yourself floating back into your body in that specific event. Really feel as if you are there. Recall the sounds, the sights and the feelings of that memory. This will bring up that resource state in you. When the emotion peaks, fill it into your chest and then pour it out of your arms into your ring of power.

Some of the states you may want in your personal ring of power are: resourcefulness, empowerment, successfulness, confidence, decisiveness, being brave, happiness, love, richness, even falling down laughing. Literally, any positive state you want to put in there is fair game.

For all the states, go through each step the same. One of the questions I have been asked when helping a person make a ring of power is "what do I do if I have never experienced the state I want?" Well, that is easy too. You can just model someone whom you think embodies that state. Let's say you have a problem recalling a past memory where you felt successful. Imagine how someone you know or know of that is successful. So if you have a friend who is successful, imagine how they feel and use that. If you don't think you know someone, then you most certainly know of someone. It could be a public figure, like Donald Trump (when he is in the billionaire phase, not filing bankruptcy), or anyone who you think well embodies that state you want.

Imagine yourself floating into their body, seeing, hearing and feeling that state just as you do with your own memories. It is very important to note that your memories are far more powerful resources than ones you get this way. So always start with the resources you have within you. They are far more abundant than you know. Now that your ring of power is fully charged it is time to test it.

Step forward into the ring of power and feel those powerful resources wash over you. Of course, that ring is portable as well. Step out of the ring and reach down to the ring and symbolically fold it in half. Then continue folding until it is small enough to put in your pocket and put it in there. You do not actually need a pocket; just symbolically put it in a virtual pocket. Any time you need these resources again, just take the ring out of your pocket and step into it. This is now your resource; you can use it anytime you need it. At this point, you are not done; you can continue improving your ring of power.

Whenever a useful state comes up, charge the ring up with those states. This ring will just get stronger and more useful the more states you anchor to it. When you need or want it, unfold it, put in on the ground and step in. when you are done, fold it back up and put it back in your pocket until next time.

One of the most common places to find misplaced anchors is food. Millions of people are eating comfort foods to improve their mood or make them feel in some way better. Unfortunately these foods are neither comfortable nor food.

This would be an example of positive anchors that are associated with unhealthy things. When a person with this feels increased pressure, stress or is just feeling like something is missing, they reach for the food that has the strongest positive anchor attached to it. These anchors often begin developing in childhood.

Parents, grandparents and other loved ones start giving sweets and sodas as a reward for something the child did well. Over time, an anchor gets set up where those foods are associated with the feelings of accomplishment and success.

Society and the media increase this with advertising and marketing campaigns that show people that are happy because they have the junk food. Of course, they always show healthy, skinny people consuming all those empty calories as well. This can set up sabotage at the unconscious level, where the unconscious mind is craving these foods to help the person lose weight, when the exact opposite is taking place.

Another anchor can be set up where a plate with food on it is a trigger to keep eating. Considering that most restaurants put enough food on one plate for two or even three people, this can be a significant problem. This is especially true when people go home and put the same amount of food on their plate there as well. This anchor usually starts with the statement that we should "clear our plate," rather than simply stop eating when we are satisfied that we have had enough food.

Ronald Berg is a certified Master of NLP, Time Techniques, and certified trainer of NLP and licensed Doctor of Chiropractic. His background in natural health gives him a unique ability to help the whole person, body, mind and spirit. He does this by addressing the physical, emotional and nutritional needs of his clients. He is located in Auburn, California where he offers hypnosis and NLP services, training and support, as well as chiropractic care to help people breakthrough their limitations and achieve the success they want in life. He offers a complimentary health report to readers of this book. You can get your report by emailing him at ronaldberg@unleashedsuccess.com or by joining his Facebook fan page "Breakthrough Unlimited" and sending him a message there. Enter code "breaking through" on the email or Facebook message.

CHAPTER NINE

Making Your Goals SMART
by Dr. Cesar Vargas

One of the most important uses of the principles of NLP is to achieve goals. More than mere goal-setting, in my Certain Goals workshops we focus on Goal GETTING. You see, we set our goals with our conscious mind, but we accomplish them (or not accomplish them) with our unconscious mind.

Truly, you can have ANYTHING you want in life, as long as you want it congruently, and you have no doubts or contradictory thinking.

There is a difference between wants and needs. A human being has certain things that they need. Psychologist Abraham Maslow developed a pyramid or hierarchy of needs. All of us find ourselves somewhere on this pyramid at different times in our lives.

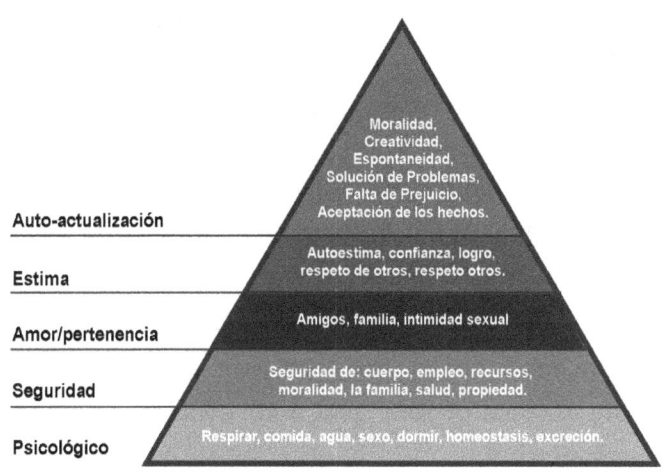

The premise of Maslow's Hierarchy of Needs is that we cannot advance to the next level until we have satisfied the needs at the lower levels. It is possible to get stuck on a particular level, which can create frustration and anxiety in our lives.

Let's see how we can utilize the way the mind works to transcend to the next level.

For instance, suppose a person is having problems with relationships, cannot keep a job and has been evicted from a number of places. This person cannot hope to begin working on the love/belonging level, if they have not dealt with the lower levels of safety and physiological issues.

In order to achieve these goals, and be sure you accomplish them with the natural help of your unconscious mind, you should make sure that your goals are SMART:

S	=	Specific / Simple
M	=	Measurable / Meaningful to you
A	=	Achievable / As if now / All areas of your life
R	=	Realistic / Responsible (Ecological)
T	=	Time-specific / Toward what you want

Specific

To your unconscious mind, a nebulous goal doesn't mean anything. The more specific your goal is, the more likely it is that you will accomplish it, because your mind has an image to go towards. It's like having a target with a bull's-eye in the center. There is just a small circle in the middle of much larger concentric circles. You want your goal to be this defined, by focusing on the essence of your goal, and reducing it down to its most essential representation.

Goals that are stated in a short phrase are much more powerful; they should be straightforward and emphasize what you want to happen, as opposed to what you don't want to happen.

Some of the things you may want to consider when creating a specific goal are:

How? How are you going to accomplish your goal?

_____

_____

Why? Why is it important for you to accomplish your goal?

_____

_____

What will the goal do for you in your life? Does it fulfill a need or want?

_____

_____

What? What are you going to do to accomplish your goal? What tools and techniques will you use? What will you accomplish once you reach your goal?

_____

_____

The more clear and concise your goals are the more likely and the more rapidly you will reach your goals. It's like playing golf. The object is to get the ball in the cup. That's the goal of golf. In order to do this, you must hold and position your golf club in a certain way. Whichever way you point your club is the way the ball will travel. There are traps and challenges along the way, but as long as you are sure of where your goal is, as long as you have a specific outcome in your mind, you can always make adjustments along the way, and eventually reach it. The more direct the route, the easier it is to find.

Simple

In NLP, we talk about your unconscious mind resembling a five-year-old genie. It's powerful enough to grant you every wish you have, provided you follow the rest of the criteria described here, but you must keep the requests clear and simple.

What is it you want, really? How would you explain what you want to a five-year-old?

If you say you want to be successful, what does that even mean? Your unconscious mind doesn't really process that, and it doesn't make sense. Additionally, to one person, success may mean not having to work on a job they don't like; to another, it may mean living in a certain city or neighborhood; to yet another, success may be having a loving family that enjoys spending time together.

The "nebulous" concept of success must be translated into a simple and concise representation. And, so it is with *love, wealth, happiness, fulfillment,* and every other goal you have. Remember the K.I.S.S. principle: Keep It Simple, Sweetheart!

Measurable

The more measureable a goal is, the easier it is to determine how close you are to attaining it. When you measure a goal, you can manage it. Your goal statement is a measure of what you want to accomplish. If you have certain measurable parameters, and you meet them, then you've accomplished your goal; it is a clear measure of success. If you're having trouble making sure your goal is measurable, you can have some short-term goals within your larger goal, which you can use as markers along the way.

Let's suppose you want a specific type of job. The first sub-goal is looking online and finding the jobs that match your skills. Then, your next sub-goal is getting your updated resume out to these companies. Then, the next sub-goal is receiving a call for an interview, then for a second interview; and your final sub-goal is that you have landed the job that you wanted.

The most important thing you can do to achieve your goals is to create a list of these smaller goals, that will lead you to your desired outcome, and NLP will help you break down any barriers along the way.

If you say, "I want a job," that statement may not be measureable. If, instead, you say, "I want a job that pays $100,000 a year and has three weeks of paid vacation with a great healthcare plan and bonuses," that is much more measureable. It is specific, and it is also something that you know you have achieved, when the criteria have been met. The more specific the criteria are towards achieving your goal (for example, paid vacations and a certain salary level), the more you will ensure that you are going after that specific goal, with those specific details that you hope to accomplish.

Meaningful to you

One of the prime directives of your unconscious mind is that it takes everything personally. Your goals should give YOU pleasure and fulfillment. Even if you're working for others, an important part of that achievement must be meaningful to you.

Meaningful to you also means tangible. I always smile to myself when I hear the classical answer from the Miss Universe contestants as to their goals when they say, "World Peace."

Your unconscious mind doesn't really know what "World Peace" means. It's a foreign concept, far too removed to be understood. If you DO, consciously, want to work on "World Peace," what you must do is translate that insubstantial phrase into something that is Meaningful to you, such as "My community gets along, and my fellow neighbors share their resources," or something similar.

As if now

When you set your goals, remember that your unconscious mind has no experience of time tenses, other than the present. There is no practical concept for the past or the future. When you remember something from the past, such as a traumatic event, what you're actually doing is bringing those memories into the present and reliving them in the here and now. That's why they hurt. If they were in the past (meaning they're over and done with), you would not hurt when you remember them.

However, don't take my word for it. Experience this yourself.

Do you have a memory of a "less than positive" experience from the past that, when you remember it, no longer bothers you? That is something that is in your practical past—it's done.

Now, if you were to remember an experience that still bothers you, you may notice that you're actually bringing the memory into the present and reliving it.

Stop it.

The best thing about the past is that it's over.

The point I'm making here is that you can only experience the present. So, when you write your goals, you must write them as if they are happening right now.

Think about it. If you write, "I will make $1,000,000" next week the instructions to your unconscious mind are "I will make $1,000,000" and next month your unconscious will continue with "I will make $1,000,000", and the year after that your unconscious is thinking "I will make $1,000,000" because the fulfillment of the goal is always in the future. Think about the beam of light on the headlights of a car; no matter how fast the car goes, it will never reach the headlight beam because it's always out in front.

Write your goals in the present tense, "as if now" you have your goal. Your unconscious mind understands this practically.

Achievable

Do not set yourself up for failure. Of course, we want you to push yourself beyond your normal expectations, but you have to make sure you can actually achieve the goal you set for yourself. Setting up unrealistic goals not only makes them impossible to attain, but it also can damage your confidence for setting and accomplishing future goals.

Setting achievable goals also helps motivate your unconscious mind to accomplish them; you can come up with ways to make your dreams a reality. You will then develop your positive attitude and outlook, because you know that the goals are within your reach. This positive outlook helps you see opportunities clearly when they present themselves to you. Your unconscious mind can help direct you, because you will be listening to your intuition and following your own inner guidance.

The problem with setting unachievable goals is that you will not be very motivated. You will listen more closely to the voice of the Chatter in your mind than you will to your unconscious mind. You will begin to develop an attitude and a habit of failure, which, in effect, will program your unconscious mind to do exactly that—fail.

Suppose you are just over five feet tall, but you want to be an Air Force pilot. The height requirement for the United States Air Force pilots is 64" to 77" (5'4" to 6'5") standing, and sitting it is 33" to 40" (2'9" to 3'4"). So, unless you are under 18 years of age and still expect a growth spurt, the goal of becoming a pilot is not achievable. However, if you want to be a commercial airline or freight pilot, this may be more achievable, as there are different height requirements for obtaining a commercial pilot's license. If it is just the Air Force you are interested in, you can still look for other careers within the USAF that do not have the height restrictions of combat pilots.

The more achievable a goal is the more likely it is that you will work hard to attain it. If you know that losing 50 lbs. in a month is not achievable, then the likelihood of losing any weight will be slim (pun intended). However, if you are looking to lose one to two pounds a week, this type of goal is much more achievable.

All Areas of Your Life

You are a multifaceted and multitalented human being. As such, you have many areas that make up your life. In order to live a balanced and fulfilled life, your goals and your growth must take place in all of these areas.

Have you ever known someone who is great at his or her relationships, but their finances are fickle? Do you know of people who are extremely religious, but their health leaves much to be desired? They may excel in one area, but neglect other areas of their lives.

Truly successful and satisfied people have goals for all areas of their lives. Now, I did mention earlier that your goal needs to be specific. So, when you write your goals, write a goal that is specific to that area of your life, and be certain to write goals for each area of your life. Consider what you'd like your life to be in your finances, your relationships, your spirituality, your health, your friends, etc.

Realistic

Being realistic is similar to assuring yourself your goal is achievable. This indicates whether a goal is actually doable by you. You might have an achievable goal but it may not be doable by you. This is the difference between possible and probable. It is possible to do many different things in life, but that does not mean that they are all probable to occur. It is possible to win the lottery. Every ticket has the same chance of winning on any given day.

However, it's just not probable that you will win the lottery. Setting unrealistic goals can be as bad as setting unachievable goals.

Realistically, you could still motivate and push yourself to reach for your dreams, but 'to thine own self be true,' wrote The Bard. And, Shakespeare must have known something about the mind mechanics of success because his plays were filled with the philosophy behind life. In the real world, if you are not honest with yourself, the consequences can be fatal.

For instance, suppose you want to become a doctor. It is definitely something that is achievable. Many people become doctors, but suppose you are not very good in math and science. You might be able to get through medical school, but is it even realistic? How much math is involved with medical school? What is likely to happen is that you will struggle a lot and may not achieve your goal, because you may have constant 'defeatist' thoughts, because you just may not be able to pass the math classes.

If something is achievable (within the realm of possibility) there are ways you can make a goal more realistic. Perhaps you can get extra tutoring in math or enter a different career within the medical field that does not require as much math. Psychiatrists require more math than psychologists. LPN's require less math than the RN's.

Make a plan on how to make the goal more realistic. Then, consider where you are in life at this moment in your life. That's becoming aware of your "here-and-now" reality.

It is difficult for some to imagine buying a $1,000,000 home if they are in a job making $37,000 a year. So, you can either change the value of the home you are looking for or push yourself towards getting a better-paying job. Either of these solutions will make the goal more realistic.

Still, set the bar high enough to make sure you are satisfied with your achievement. However, if the goal is too high, and you fail you will not feel very successful.

If, on the other hand, you are aiming for goals that are beneath your skill level, even if you achieve the goal, you may not feel very satisfied with the experience. You also may not feel that you have advanced in your attainment, or that you are even successful. Consider the bull's-eye. If you can shoot an arrow fairly well, and you are only standing 2 feet from the target, you might easily hit the bull's-eye. However, it won't be very satisfying to you. On the other hand, if you stand across a field, your goal is more achievable, and it will stretch your skills somewhat, but it is still realistic for most people. However, if you blindfold yourself, the goal can still be achievable, but not really realistic.

NLP techniques can open up new possibilities for you. What you may have thought was unachievable or unrealistic can become possible. Many times, it is your own fears and doubts that can obscure goals or even make them unachievable. Once you remove the fears, your goals become very achievable. When you begin to achieve things that you once thought impossible, your confidence will increase simultaneously. It opens up far greater possibilities for you. You are building on your successes, and you're taking your life to the next level of achievement.

Responsible (Ecological)

To be Responsible or Ecological, in this sense, means that, in setting your goals, you consider your own well being, the well being of all those involved, the well being of your community, and the well being of the world.

Deep in your unconscious mind, there is a part that is looking out for ecology. If your goal is to make a million dollars, but you have to sell inferior products to people, you're much less likely to achieve that, because you're violating your Ecological check.

You may say, "But there are people out there who are doing things that are not ecological." True. But how truly successful are they in the long run? Sooner or later, they will be found out and brought to justice, and they never really enjoyed true success and satisfaction, anyway.

Time specific

Setting the right time frame is very important in achieving goals. Remember the example of losing 50 pounds in one month. This timeframe is neither attainable nor realistic, and this is because of the timeframe involved. People lose fifty pounds all the time. They just do it over a reasonable amount of time.

Also, it is important to set a time in your goal-making. This helps keep you on track and have an arrival time. When you book a flight to a destination, you usually look at when the plane lands. If you did not see an arrival time, this might make you a little nervous. Will the plane just be flying around aimlessly? Are there other destinations along the way? Will the pilot land the plane for awhile to take a nap? Knowing when you are going to arrive at a destination is important.

Setting a time for you to achieve your goal becomes a promise you make to yourself that you will reach it. If you tell someone that you will meet them at 2:00 tomorrow, then you are making a promise to them. When 2:00 rolls around, the expectation is that you will meet at the agreed-upon location. Setting a time for a goal is similar. You are saying that on a certain date, and maybe even a specific time, you will arrive at your goal.

If you do not set a time for your goal, then this can be too vague. Consider the example above. If you told your friend that you would meet them sometime this week, then they would not have an expectation that they would ever see you, except by accident.

Some time ago, I heard the story of Mae Laborde, a 101-year-old actress (born May 13, 1909) who did a series of commercials for the Fox Network and the FX channel. The most astonishing fact about Mae's story is that she started in the acting business at the age of 93! In an interview, she said that she "always wanted to do this" (acting).

She had a goal to become an actress—perhaps it was even her passion—, but she never made her goal time-specific. It is imperative that your goal be specific as to the time, otherwise you may get the achievement of your goal, but much later than you imagine. What if you had a goal to meet the love of your life? You go through your entire life without meeting that special someone. Then, on your deathbed, you finally see in the eyes of your nurse that spark you were always looking for. "Your wish is my command." It's been granted, but a bit too late to enjoy fully.

Without setting a time on your goal, there will be no urgency to achieve it. It would mean you could start any time and arrive anytime. The likelihood of you arriving at your goal would be by pure chance alone.

Like other aspects of goal-setting, setting a time must be realistic and achievable. If you give yourself too much time, you may become distracted or bored, and not be too motivated to take action now. Suppose you want to start your own business. If you say in the next five years you might want to open your own business, you might not be motivated to do what it takes to get there. If, on the other hand, the time is too short, such as "next week I want to be in operation," this may not be realistic or achievable, as you may need to get a business license, select a product or service, create a business plan, etc.

Toward what you want

There are two basic types of motivation that drive everything we do: Pain and Pleasure. We seek to avoid pain and to gain pleasure. In NLP, these are known as Propulsion Systems.

If you've ever seen a rocket launch to the Moon, it is an impressive sight to behold. After the countdown reaches zero, the rumble of the solid rocket boosters fills the air, and an impressive 7.8 million pounds of thrust overcomes gravity's pull, launching the spacecraft to about 18,000 miles per hour. The initial force to escape Earth's gravity is immense. However, that's not all.

After the spacecraft leaves the Earth's atmosphere, it takes very little to maintain speed. After a while, as the spacecraft comes closer to the Moon, our satellite's gravitational force actually pulls the spacecraft toward it.

It's the same thing with our goals. You can have two foci in any particular goal. If the area of your life you're working on is relationships, you can have a goal to meet the person who will be your partner for life.

Within that goal, it is essential to know *why* you want that relationship. Is it to enjoy life and share your gifts and talents with another person, or is it so you won't be lonely?

Do you notice the difference?

In the first *reason*, you're moving towards something you want (sharing of yourself with another human being), while in the other *reason* your focus is away from what you don't want (to be lonely).

At first, this may take some introspection and honesty on your part. You can't just say, "Yes, I want to share my life with another person" only because you just read that. Again, "To thine own self be true." What is the *real* reason that YOU want to have that relationship?

It's important to know, because the focus of your work will be different in each case. Imagine if the space shuttle crew would simply wait at the launch pad for the Moon's gravitational pull to do its thing. Nothing would ever happen!

In order to be truly successful and motivated to achieve your goals, it is essential that you define your Toward and Away From motivators. The best strategy is to use a combination of both. First, the Away From motivation needs to be strong enough to overcome inertia—the cost of doing nothing. Then, once you're far away from the thing that got you moving in the first place, you engage the Toward motivation to pull you to your optimal life.

At the end of this chapter is a worksheet that we use in my Goals Seminars, and I provide to my private clients, which serves as a reminder of, and a primer for the elements of a SMART goal.

Using the SMART method, while utilizing NLP techniques, can move mountains for you. You will be amazed how easily you can achieve the goals you may have been trying to achieve your entire life to achieve, without success.

Write goals for each area of your life, and use this SMART goal worksheet to be sure to include all these factors.

Cesar Vargas, Ph.D. is a Doctor of Clinical Hypnotherapy with a thriving Coaching Practice and an International Training Company in the areas of Success, Achievement and Human Development. He is the author of *Your Life Is Your Masterpiece* (www.YourLifeIsYourMasterpiece.com), co-author of *Descubre TU Grandeza* (*Discover YOUR Greatness*), and translator into Spanish of Joe Vitale's *Spiritual Marketing*, Karol Truman's *Feelings Buried Alive, Never Die*, James Arthur Ray's *The Science of Success* and *Practical Spirituality*, Bart Baggett's *Success Secrets of the Rich and Happy*, and Wallace D. Wattles' *Science of Getting Rich* and Michael Stevenson's *Learn Hypnosis... Now!* He also presents workshops in some of these topics around the country and throughout the world. His main website is www.MenteInc.com, where you can get a complimentary 15-minute consultation. You may also contact him on Facebook at www.facebook.com/cesartrance

SMART Goal Worksheet

S Specific
    Simple

M Measurable
    Meaningful to you

A As if now
    Achievable
    All areas of your life

R Realistic
    Responsible / Ecological

T Timed
    Toward What You Want

_____
_____
_____
_____
_____
_____
_____

CHAPTER TEN

Tapping into Success
by Michael Stevenson

What is EFT?

EFT, or Emotional Freedom Techniques, is a therapy technique loosely based on the techniques of acupuncture or acupressure. It uses the same basic energy meridians in the body to eliminate physical, emotional and mental issues.

EFT balances the energy system of the body to relieve our own issues. It is safe, easy and fun, and can help you release those things that block you from happiness, love, health, wealth and other wonderful things in life.

It's based on a more complex technique called TFT or Thought Field Therapy, created by Roger Callahan. EFT founder Gary Craig realized, after taking Callahan's course, that he could greatly simplify the procedure.

Gary taught EFT for more than two decades and provided thousands of people with the key to unlock the shackles of mediocrity in their life. Gary Craig's entire EFT manual is available as a free download from emofree.com.

Effectiveness of EFT

EFT is effective for relieving physical, emotional, mental and energetic blocks. It has been proven effective for everything from minor habits like nail-biting to major habits like smoking and drug addictions, from minor pains like arthritis to chronic pain, or from minor emotions like fears to major phobias.

As a matter of fact, EFT is so effective. The mantra in the field is, "try it on everything." It takes only 90 seconds or so to do one round of EFT, so give it a shot!

Why EFT Works for Success

There are two components to attracting wealth into your life. I refer to them as, "The Big U's." I often capitalize them, because they're that important. One is internal, and one is external.

The first is that you are a person of two minds. Your conscious mind is the part you think with. It is the logical, protective part of you that analyzes the environment and makes decisions. It's the part of your mind that you set your goals with — your "goal setter."

However, your Unconscious mind is more important to the process of goal getting. Your unconscious mind is the emotive, imaginative, creative part of you, where all your memories, beliefs, values and lessons are stored. Your unconscious mind automatically moves you toward your goals when it is in alignment. It is your "goal getter."

The problems arise when you get out of alignment. If your conscious mind says "I want more money," but your Unconscious mind says, "Rich people are greedy," you'll have a deep unconscious need not to achieve that goal, because you don't want to be evil. It goes against your unconscious values. No matter what you do consciously, you'll sabotage those results.

How it works

Imagine you took the back off your TV set. Inside, you would see wires, electronics, circuit boards, etc.

If you were to jam a screwdriver inside those electronics, you would disrupt the flow of the energy, and the TV would go "Zzzzt!" and the picture would fuzz out.

That's the same thing that happens in your body when you experience a negative emotion.

EFT states that, "The cause of all negative emotions is a disruption of the body's energy system.

To experience a negative emotion, we have a negative experience, or a distressing memory. The energy system gets disrupted, and then we feel that disruption, calling it a "negative emotion."

To balance this system, all we have to do is "tune into" the energy of the problem, and then balance that disruption.

The Basic Recipe

Just like baking a cake, with EFT, you have a recipe. And it's a very simple recipe.

The recipe consists of just three rounds.
1. The Setup
2. The Sequence
3. The Suggestions

While older versions of EFT had more steps, this new, streamlined version is actually easier to use and more effective.

The key to EFT is not necessarily technique, but persistence.

Before you start the process, always get a gauge of the problem on a scale from zero to ten. This helps show the progress with each round of tapping.

The Setup

The Setup is vital to the whole process and prepares the energy system so that the rest of The Basic Recipe can do its job.

The Setup is designed to make sure your energy system is properly oriented before attempting to remove its disruptions and corrects "Psychological Reversal," or a "Polarity Reversal" of the energy system.

Psychological Reversal is a reversal of the energy system in the body. Just as putting batteries in a remote control backwards will not work, your own energy system will not work property if the polarity is reversed.

It is because of Psychological Reversal (PR) that some diseases are chronic and respond poorly to conventional treatments. PR is, quite literally, the cause of self-sabotage and sabotaging emotions. It creates self-defeating thinking and behavior, so we must correct for it.

It begins with an affirmation while tapping on the karate chop point on the side of your hand:

"Even though I have this (problem), I deeply and completely accept myself."

To perform the setup, repeat this phrase three times while tapping the karate chop point on the side of either hand.

The Sequence

The EFT sequence is a highly-optimized version of the TFT tapping points. Rather than doing hours of muscle testing to discover where to tap, just tap them all – it only takes a minute! The points are:

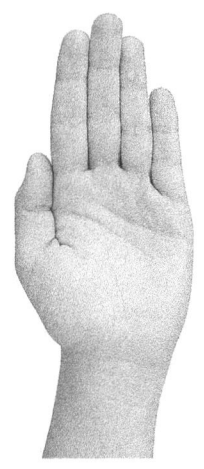

Golpe de Karate

- Eyebrow (EB)
- Side of the Eye (SE)
- Ender the Eye (UE)
- Under Nose (UN)
- Chin (CH)
- Collar Bone (CB)
- Under Arm (UA)
- Top of Head (TH)

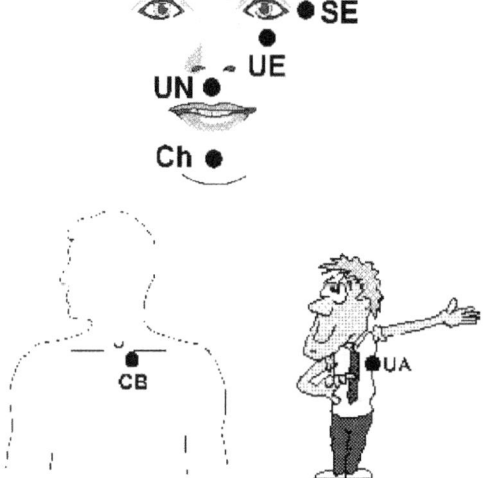

Each time you tap the point, tap it seven to ten times, each time repeating the name of the problem that you specified in The Setup. For instance "this headache, this headache, this headache."

The Suggestions

This part of the recipe is just like the last, except that rather than repeating the problem; you repeat positive suggestions for each point. Again, the points are:

- Eyebrow (EB)
- Side of the Eye (SE)
- Ender the Eye (UE)
- Under Nose (UN)
- Chin (CH)
- Collar Bone (CB)
- Under Arm (UA)
- Top of Head (TH)

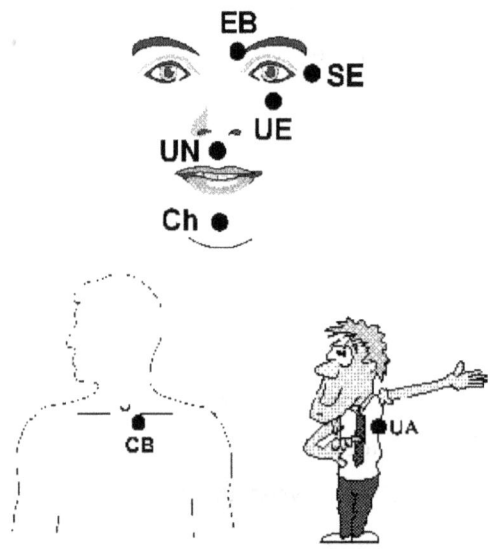

Each time you tap the point, tap it seven to ten times, each time giving positive suggestions. For instance, "My head feels wonderful, I am calm and rested, I go through the day in control of my feelings, etc."

Subsequent Rounds

In many cases, EFT will eliminate a pain, emotion or fear with one or two rounds. If repeated rounds don't completely eliminate the problem, there are two tracts you can take.

Focus on the remaining Problem

Run the basic recipe again; this time focusing specifically on the remaining problem.

The Setup: *"Even though I still have some of this (problem), I deeply and completely accept myself."*

The Sequence: *"This remaining (problem)."*

Focus on aspects

For each problem, there can be many different aspects. For instance, PTSD can often be fed by many different memories. You may have to do the basic recipe on each memory until it gets to zero to eliminate the problem.

Phobias can have different aspects. Someone with a water phobia may not be able to get within 100 ft. of a pool. After you tap on the problem, they may be able to get 10 ft from the pool before having the response. Tap on *that* problem as another aspect. Then, they may be able to only go in up to their knees. Tap on that as an aspect, until the entire phobia is gone.

Michael Stevenson is a certified trainer, therapist and coach in Orange County, California.

This chapter is an excerpt from Michael's Book, Tapping into Wealth with EFT, available at www.transformdestiny.com

BONUS CHAPTER

A Final Review and Your Call to Action

by Cesar Vargas, Ph.D.

Now you have everything you need, and more, to get your life Unstuck and create the life you haven't even dreamed of, full of possibilities and achievements. It's time to Take Action immediately. In my Goal-Setting courses, one of the commitments successful people make is to DO SOMETHING within the first 24 hours of setting a goal toward the achievement of that goal.

I'm sure you've set goals before that you didn't take action on, and therefore didn't get. If that's the case, you've habituated your Subconscious mind to your Daydreaming State.

But, when you actually Take Action... swift, immediate and directed action... it's like a jolt to your Subconscious mind, which thinks, "Oh, this is real, now. This is NOT Daydreaming... We're actually going for this. Great!"

So, decide NOW what are you going to do within the next 24 hours toward getting your Life Unstuck Now. Then DO IT. Schedule it! Put it on your Crackberry(NOT-TM) / youPhone(NOT-TM) or other scheduling device and actually DO IT!

Remember, successful people make lots of decisions, make their decisions quickly, and they stick to them until they complete them. Because you're a successful person, you are now going to schedule and achieve your success... you're going to get your Life Unstuck Now! Step out of your Comfort Zone and Go For It! Keep in mind that "By expanding your comfort zone, you will expand the size of your income and wealth zone."

Keep yourself At Cause for everything that happens in your life, and everything that comes into your awareness. Find out what motivates you, and DO THAT. Are you more motivated to go for the things you want, or to avoid the things you don't want? Capitalize on that!

Practice getting in rapport with others, for fun and profit. It's easy, and it just requires daily practice in matching and mirroring. Take charge of your life by tapping into your highest values, and tying your outcomes to those values. Put your outcomes and goals into perspective by choosing the right chunk size for immediate and powerful action, and tune your own Personal TV for maximum desire for those goals and outcomes... Make them Irresistible and Compelling.

Identify states and anchors that are setting you back and/or keeping you stuck, and create new, empowering anchors that propel you toward what you want. Continue to build upon your Personal Ring of Power, and add positive, powerful and empowering states to them constantly.

Set your goals and make them S.M.A.R.T., and create goals for every area of your life. Then... Take ACTION!

And, as you go through your life, success after success, should you encounter the need to tap away at the stress and the anxiety, now you have the tools to do just that. DO try it on everything. I assure you you'll be pleasantly surprised.

I want to hear from you.

Please contact me on Facebook or my main website.

So, I wonder what you will do with your life now that you're Unstuck!

I wish you Massive Success!

Cesar Vargas, Ph.D.

ORDER FORM ON NEXT PAGE

ORDER FORM

I'd like to get additional copies of **Un-Stuck: The Owner's Manual for Success** for me and/or my family, friends and others who are about to get unstuck in their lives.

Name: _____

Address: _____

City: _____ State: _____

Country: _____ Zip: _____

Email (for confirmation): _____

Comments (additional on reverse): _____

Quantity _____ X $12.95 (USD)   **Subtotal $**_____

S&H   USA and Canadá $ 7.50
             Latin America $ 12.50
             Rest of the World   Ask

Email: info@lifeunstucknow.com

Total Enclosed (USD) $_____

Send this Order Form with your payment to:

VERITAS INVICTUS PUBLISHING
8502 East Chapman Avenue # 302
Orange, California 92869
United States

To get it over the Internet with your credit card, go to:
www.lifeunstucknow.com